PLANET NEWS

1961 - 1967

ALLEN GINSBERG

*'O go way man I can
   hypnotize this nation
I can shake the earth's foundation
   with the Maple Le   '*

City Lights Books

Fifteenth printing: January 2013

ISBN-13: 978-0-87286-020-5

ISBN: 0-87286-020-5
Library of Congress Catalog Card #68-25477

CITY LIGHTS BOOKS are edited by Lawrence Ferlinghetti and
Nancy J. Peters and published at the City Lights Bookstore,
261 Columbus Avenue, San Francisco, CA 94133.

Visit our Website: http://www.citylights.com

Dedicated

to

Neal Cassady
again

Spirit to Spirit

February 8, 1925 — February 4, 1968

' the greater driver '
' secret hero of these poems '

Acknowledgements : These poems were printed first (in forms slightly closer to original composition, i.e. there has been some revision for syntactical condensation toward directer presentation of the original spontaneous imagery, a method similar to manicuring grass that is removal of seeds and twigs, ands, buts, ors especially ofs that don't contribute to getting the mind high) in *Wild Dog, Brown Paper,* Columbia *Jester, TV Baby Poems* (Cape-Golliard London 67), *Ramparts, Bugger (Fuck You/a Magazine of the Arts* supplement), *League for Sexual Freedom* leaflet series, *Gnaoua, Jerusalem Post, Burning Bush, Salted Feathers, Four Seasons, Residu, Fuck You/A Magazine of the Arts, 'C', Kulcher, Ice & Frice, My Own Mag, The World,* lower *Eastside Review, The Yale Literary Magazine, Auerhahn/Haselwood* tinybooks, *Oyez* poster, *Evergreen Review, Isis, Wholly Communion, Something, Los Angeles Free Press, Cranium Press* Broadsides, *Now, Scrip Magazine, Village Voice, Berkeley Barb, Peace News, Life, Quixote, Hika, Coyote, The Sunflower* (Wichita State), *Fifth Estate, Do-it, Grist, Desert Review, Synapse, Nadada, Paris Review, Liberation News Service, Writer's Forum, Underdog, rhinozeros, Mahenjodaro, Il Tarocco, Che Fare, Planeta Fresca, Klacto 23, Poets at Le Metro, Notes from the Garage Door, American Dialogue, Playboy, Win, The New Yorker,* & else where?

— A.G.

Acknowledgement Addenda : fellow poet Charles Plymell helped clean up, complete, name & photoprint *Television Was A Baby Crawling Toward That Deathchamber* for public eyes; friend poet Lawrence Ferlinghetti encouraged book to finish, suggested additions & style edited *Planet News.*

CONTENTS

Who Will Take Over the Universe?

A bitter cold winter night
conspirators at cafe tables
            discussing mystic jails
The Revolution in America
        already begun not bombs but sit
            down strikes on top submarines
        on sidewalks nearby City Hall —
How many families control the States?
        Ignore the Government,
            send your protest to Clint Murchison.
The Indians won their case with Judge McFate
                Peyote safe in Arizona —
        In my room the sick junky
                    shivers on the 7th day
                Tearful, reborn to the Winter.
Che Guevara has a big cock
                Castro's balls are pink —
The Ghost of John F. Dulles hangs
            over America like dirty linen
        draped over the wintery red sunset,
        Fumes of Unconscious Gas
                emanate from his corpse
            & hypnotize the Egyptian intellectuals —
He grinds his teeth in horror & crosses his
                thigh bones over his skull
        Dust flows out of his asshole
            his hands are full of bacteria
                The worm is at his eye —
He's declaring counterrevolutions in
                    the Worm-world,

my cat threw him up last
                    Thursday.
& Forrestal flew out his window like an Eagle —
America's spending money to overthrow the Man.
                Who are the rulers of the earth?

January 6, 1961

JOURNAL NIGHT THOUGHTS

NY January 1961

In bed on my green purple pink
    yellow orange bolivian blanket,
the clock tick, my back against the wall
— staring into black circled eyes magician
    man's bearded glance & story
the kitchen spun in a wheel of vertigo,
the eye in the center of the moving
        mandala — the
        eye in the hand
        the eye in the asshole
        serpent eating or
          vomiting its tail
— the blank air a solid wall revolving
    around my retina —
The wheel of jewels and fire I saw moving
        vaster than my head in Peru
Band circling in band and a black
        hole of Calcutta thru which
        I stared at my Atman
          without a body —
The Giotto window on Boston giving
        to a scene in Bibled Palestine
        A golden star
        and the flight to Egypt
          in an instant now
Come true again — the Kabbala sign
    in the vomit on the floor —
From a window on Riverside Drive,

Lower East Side
2 Street
High

★

W / Harry Smith

★

Optical
Phenomena

★

Yage
in
Pucallpa

★

Remembering
Leary's Bedroom
Harvard

★

Jack
Hallucinating

★

10

one boat moving slowly
up the flowing river, small autos
crawling on Hudson Thruway
       a plash of white snow on
         the Palisades
and a small white park etched
  by bare thin branches
with black birds aflutter in the
         frosty underbrush
Riverside Drive, as in Breughel
  a girl in red coat
      — a footprint, a lone
        passerby
on sidewalk under apartment wall —
and a blimp from the war floating in air
  over the edge of the city —
Wagner's last echoes, and Baudelaire
  inscribing his oceanic page
    of confessions
Ah love is so sweet in the Springtime
      Amor Vincit Omnia
Eliot's voice clanging over the sky
    on upper Broadway
" Only thru Time is Time conquered "
I am the answer : I will swallow my
  vomit and be naked —
A heavy rain, the plick of a raindrop
      shattered on the fire escape rail
        at the level of my eye —
This woman is a serpent goddess accepting
  the propitiation of a bunch of flowers
  found in the Christmas snow

*Out Robt.
Lowell's Window*

★

*Unsteadily
Walking
in
Manhattan
Near Where
Poe Wrote
The
Raven*

★

*Visiting
Dorothy Norman*

★

on Mad. Ave. dusk uptown —
We'll rush around in a redcross psychic
aumbulance past the Museum of
Natural History
delivering Anxiety mushrooms to the dancing
red gummed skeletons
their lifted legs are crossed
they wear iron crowns
The cat vomited his canned food with a
mix of inch-long worms
that arched up over the
dread plop —
I threw it in the garbage bag aghast —
cockroach crawls up the bath tub Yosemite wall,
rust in the hot water faucet, a sweet smell
in the mouldy chicken soup,
and little black beings in the old bag of flour
on the pantry shelf last week
Natchez, he was saying with his head one side
of the center of the wheel
of Vertigo —
burned babies in the blaze of a fiery house
sending them back to the Sun —
They drank a black elixir, and threw it up
To have the serpent intertwined
in their eyeballs —
One man was born with genitals all over
his body — there were 15,000,000
Indians in North America then —
The mushroom image in the Spiro Mound
The battle with the two-headed
caterpillar big as a house

Psylocibin Taxi

★

*The Citipati
(Tibetan Bones)*

★

*Housecat
in the
Slums*

★

*Smith's
Anthropological
Gossip*

★

with waving lobster claws —
Here is the Homunculus wavering in the brain,
      the aggregate of ignorant patterns
                  looking like Denny Dimwit

*Penfield's
Homunculus*

★

The genitals are larger than the head —
      huge thumbs, and the crab image
            of the back of the mouth —
'Twas a sunflower-monkey on Neptune
      I imagined over the radio —

*Ditty
Taped at Jack's*
★

Somebody's got to make a break & contact
      Khruschev in the Nöosphere —
because I took a sick crap near a skull
      with long red hair in a coastal desert
            gravepit by the Peruvian Pacific —
across the road, new green fields and hut trees
and now I'm paranoiac every day about the cops
                        (& god & universe)

*Historic
Paranoia
From
Boston
To
Lima*

★

      as if it were all being tape recorded from my
            skull to project the Kali Yuga —
He saw electric wires on the floor — He saw
      the channel that heard yr mind
            thru the music —
I saw the flower, slowly awakening its petals —
My face in the hot dog stand mirror
      harried to be here again
to see myself alive on Broadway afraid I'm
      in a forgotten movie where I die
            not knowing my name —

*Back In
Memory City*

★

The old man came out of his room Carpet
            slippers, getting bald
with half a sheaf of indecipherable arrangements

*A Retired
Schoolteacher
In
Newark:*

of words in singsong
" rain in heart by heat a fool be clang "
Cerebral stroke stiff hand
His tongue stopped forever
but his mind went on
in what universe?

*Visit To
Friend of the
Family*

★

I dreamt I had to destroy the human
universe to be Messiah —

LSD Roars

My toes wiggle on the bed, the breast has
eyes and mouth,

★

the belly eye & dumb lips and the loins
a blind one waiting —
a big fart gave the void a smelly minute —
The color of the wind? It could be the same
the color of the water —
Where does rain come from? Nice to look up
at the stars in Northport —

*Gaga &
Dialogue
W/ Lafcadio*

★

'Er something. Uh-huh.
I could see the hairs at the end of his nose.
We were involved in a great tragedy together —
I walked alone, in the street, by myself
with no God to turn to

*N²O at the
Dentist*

★

But what I Am —
who can create baby universes
in the mouth of the void —
Spurt them out of my mind forever
to fill the Unimaginable with its
separate being —

*Mescaline Mouth
Ejaculations
Of Me*

★

So I left behind a message to the Consciousness
before I disappeared —

Poësy

I wrote it on a stone & left it in Oklahoma
in that Indian mound,

★

drew a picture of a serpent crossing in
    and out of its folds like a scaly
    swastika — a green dragon
        with ancient fangs —
Speak up and tell yr secret, is it a
    living animal out there your
        afraid of still — ?
And my mother's skull not yet white
    in the darkness, a glimpse of
        that forgotten creature agape
        at dirty nothing — GO
          BACK!
I come in the ass of my beloved, I lay back
    with my cock in the air to be kissed —
I prostrate my sphincter with my eyes in
    the pillow, my legs are thrown up
        over your shoulder,
I feel your buttocks with my hand
        a cock throbs I lay still my
        mouth in my ass —
I kiss the hidden mouth, I have a third eye
I paint the pupils on my palm, and an
      eyelash that winks —

*Death
Consciousness*

★

*Kaddish
Completed
" You're not done
with your mother
yet."
Sd/ Elise C.*

★

*Come To
This
End*

TELEVISION WAS A BABY CRAWLING
TOWARD THAT DEATHCHAMBER

It is here, the long Awaited bleap-blast light that Speaks one red
 tongue like Politician, but happy its own govt.,
either we blow ourselves up now and die, like the old tribe of
 man, arguing among neutrons, spit on India, fuck Tibet,
 stick up America, clobber Moscow, die Baltic, have your
 tuberculosis in Arabia, wink not in Enkidu's reverie —
it's a long Train of Associations stopped for gas in the desert &
 looking for drink of old-time H^2O —
made up of molecules, it ends being innocent as Lafcadio afraid
 to get up & cook his bacon —
I prophesy: the Pigs won't mind! I prophesy: Death will be old
 folks home!
I prophesy: Chango will prophesy on national Broadcasting System,
I prophesy, we will all prophesy to each other & I give thee
 happy tidings Robert Lowell and Jeanette MacDonald —
Dusty moonlight, Starbeam riding its own flute, soul revealed in
 the scribble, an ounce of looks, an Invisible Seeing, Hope,
 The Vanisher betokening Eternity
one finger raised warning above his gold eyeglasses — and
 Mozart playing giddy-note an hour on the Marxist
 gramophone —
All Be — let the Kaballah star be formed of perfect circles in a
 room of 1950 unhappiness where Myrna Loy gets lost —
The Bardo Thodol extends in the millions of black jello for every
 dying Mechanic — We will make Colossal movies —
We will be a great Tantric Mogul & starify a new Hollywood
 with our unimaginable Flop — Great Paranoia!
The Family presents, your Corpse Hour — attended by myriads

flies — hyperactive Commentators freed at their most
    bestial — sneering literary — perhaps a captive & loan
    Square

caught hiding behind a dummy-univac in the obscurest Morgues
    of Hearst — wherever — no more possible —

Only remains, a photo of a riverswollen hand in black and
    white, arm covered by aged burlap to the wrist —

skin peeling from the empty fingers —; Yet discovered by a mad
    Negro high on tea & solitary enough himself to notice a
    Fate —

therefore, with camera remembered and passed along by hand
    mail roaring Jet toward Chicago, Big Table empty this
    morning,

nothing but an old frog-looking editor worried about his
    Aesthetics,

That's life Kulchur '61 — retired to New York to invent Morse
    Code & found a great yellow Telegraph —

Merry Xmas Paul carroll and irving Rose in Thrall — give up
    thy song & flower to any passing Millennium!

I am the One, you are the One, we are the One, A. Hitler's One
    as well as fast as his Many heavenly Jews are reborn,

many a being with a nose — and many with none but an ear
    somewhere next to a Yelling Star —

I myself saw the sunflower-monkeys of the Moon — spending
    their dear play-money electricity in a homemade tape-record
    minute of cartoony high Sound —

goodbye Farewell repeated by Wagner Immortal in many a
    gladdened expanding mid-europe Hour

that I'll be hearing forever if the world I go to's Music, Yes good
    to be stuck thru Eternity on that aching Liebestod Note

which has been playing out there always for me, whoever can
    hear enough to write it down for a day to let men fiddle in

space, blow a temporary brass tuba or wave a stick at a
physical orchestra
and remember the Wagner-music in his own titty-head Con-
sciousness — ah yes that's the message —
That's what I came here to compose, what I knocked off my life
to Inscribe on my grey metal typewriter,
borrowed from somebody's lover's mother got it from Welfare,
all interconnected and gracious a bunch of Murderers
as possible in this Kalpa of Hungry blood-drunkard Ghosts —
We all have to eat — us Beings
gnaw bones, suck marrow, drink living white milk from heavenly
Breasts or from bucktoothed negress or wolf-cow.
The sperm bodies wriggle in pools of vagina, in Yin, that reality
we must have spasmd our Beings upon —
The brothers and sisters die if we live, the Myriads Invisible
squeak reptile complaint
on Memory's tail which us pterodactyl-buzzard-dove-descended
two foot mammal-born Geek-souls almost Forget —
Grab — a cock — any eye — bright hair — All Memory & All
Eternity now, reborn as One —
no loss to those — the Peacock spreads its cosmic-eye Magnificat-
feathered tail over its forgotten Ass —
The being roars its own name in the Radio, the Bomb goes off its
twenty years ago,
I hear thy music O my mystery, my Father in myself, my mother
in my eye, brother in my hand, sister-in-honey on my own
Poetry's Tongue, my Hallelujah Way beyond all mortal
inherited Heavens, O my own blind ancient Love-in-mind!
Who? but us all, a Me, a One, a Dying Being, The presence,
now, this desk, hand running over the steps of imagination
over the letter-ladders on machine, vibrating humm-herald
Extend-hope own unto Thee, returning infinite-myriad at

the Heart, that is only red blood,

that is where murder is still innocence, that life ate, the white plasmic monsters forage in their fleet Macrocosm — bit apple or black huge bacteria gods loomed out of nowhere, potent

maybe once victorious on Saturn in dinosaur-inspired messy old hallucinated war —

same battle raging in tsraved cats and gahgard dogs for American ghostly bone — man and man, fairy against red, black on white on white, with teeth going to the dentist to escape in gas —

The President laughs in his Chair, and swivels his head on his neck controlling fangs of Number —

bacteria come numberless, atoms count themselves greatness in their pointy Empire —

Russian Neutrons spy on all Conspiracy — & Chinese yellow energy waves have ocean and Empyrean ready against attack & future starvation — Korean principalities of Photon are doubles in all but name — differing Wizards of Art of Electron divide as many as tribes of Congo — Africa's a vast jail of Shadows — I am not I,

my molecules are numbered, mirrored in all Me Robot Seraphy parts, cock-creator navel-marked, Eye Seer with delicate breasts, teeth & gullet to ingest the living dove-life

foreimage of the Self-Maw Death Is Now; — but there is the Saintly Meat of the Heart — feeling to thee o Peter and all my Lords — Decades American loves car-rides and vow-sworn faces lain on my breast, — my head on many more naked than my own sad hoping flesh —

our feelings! come back to the heart — to the old blind hoping Creator home in Mercy, beating everywhere behind machine hand clothes-man Senator iron powerd or fishqueen fugitive-com'd lapel —

Here I am — Old Betty Boop whoopsing behind the skull-
microphone wondering what Idiot soap opera horror show
we broadcast by Mistake — full of communists and franken-
stein cops and

mature capitalists running the State Department and the Daily
News Editorial hypnotizing millions of legional-eyed
detectives to commit mass murder on the Invisible

which is only a bunch of women weeping hidden behind news-
papers in the Andes, conspired against by Standard Oil,

which is a big fat fairy monopolizing all Being that has form'd
it self to Oil,

and nothing gets in its way so it grabs different oils in all poor
mystic aboriginal Principalities too weak to

Screech out over the radio that Standard Oil is a bunch of
spying Businessmen intent on building one Standard Oil in
the whole universe like an egotistical cancer

and yell on Television to England to watch out for United Fruits
they got Central America by the balls

nobody but them can talk San Salvador, they run big Guatemala
puppet armies, gas Dictators, they're the Crown of Thorns

upon the Consciousness of poor Christ-indian Central America,
and the Pharisees are US Congress & Publicans is the
American People

who have driven righteous bearded faithful pink new Castro
1961 is he mad? who knows — Hope for him, he stay true

& his wormy 45-year dying peasants teach Death's beauty sugar
beyond politics, build iron children schools

for alphabet molecule stars, that mystic history & giggling
revolution henceforth no toothless martyrs be memorized by
some pubescent Juan who'll smoke my marihuana —

Turn the Teacher on! — Yes not conspire dollars under navy-
town boardwalk, not spy vast Services of gunny Secrecy

under drear eyeglass Dulles to ASSASSINATE!
INVADE! STARVE OUT! SUPPLY INVISIBLE ARMS!
GIVE MONEY TO ORGANIZE DEATH FOR CUBAN
REVOLUTION! BLOCKADE WHAT FRAIL MAC-
HINERY!
MAKE EVIL PROPAGANDA OVER THE WORLD!
ISOLATE THE FAITHFUL'S SOUL! TAKE ALL
RICHES BACK! BE WORLDLY PRINCE AND
POWER OVER THE UNBELIEVABLE! MY GOD!
AMERICA WILL BE REFUSED ETERNITY BY HER OWN
MAD SON THE BOMB! MEN WORKING IN ELEC-
TRICITY BE U.S. SADISTS THEIR MAGIC
PHANOPOEIAC THRU MASS MEDIA THE
NASTIEST IN THIS FIRST HISTORY!
EVIL SPELLS THRU THE DAILY NEWS! HORRIBLE
MASOCHISMS THUNK UP BY THE AMERICAN
MEDICAL ASSOCIATION! DEATH TO JUNKIES
THRU THE TREASURY DEPARTMENT! TAXES ON
YOUR HATE FOR THIS HERE WAR!
LEGIONS OF DECENCY BLACKMAIL THY CINEMAL
FATE! CONSPIRACIES CONTROL ALL WHITE
MAGICIANS! I CAN'T TELL YOU MY SECRET
STORY ON TV!
Chambers of Commerce misquote Bob Hope who is a grim sex
revolutionist talking in hysterical code flat awful jokes
Jimmy Durante's kept from screaming to death in the movies by
a huge fat Cardinal, the Spell Man, Black Magician he
won't let mad white Chaplin talk thru the State Mega-
phone! He takes evil pix with Swiss financial cunt!
It's the American Medical Association poisoning the poets with
their double-syndicate of heroin cut with money-dust,
Military psychiatrists make deathly uniforms it's Tanganyikan

nerve-skin in the submarinic navy they're prepared for
eternal solitude, once they go down they turn to Reptiles
Human dragons trained to fly the air with bomb-claws clutched
to breast & wires entering their brains thru muffled ears —
connected to what control tower — jacked to what secret
Lab where the macrocosm-machine
picks up vibrations of my thought in this poem — the attendant
is afraid — Is the President listening? is
Evil Eye, the invisible police-cop-secrecy masters Controlling
Central Intelligence — do they know I took Methedrine,
heroin, magic mushrooms, & lambchops & guess toward a
Prophesy tonight?
No the big dopes all they do is control each other — Doom! in
the vast
car America — they're screeching on two mind-wheels on a
National Curve — the Car that's made to die by Mr.
Inhuman
Moneyhand, by advertising nastyhead Inc. Dream Cancer Prexy
Owner Distributor Publisher & TV Doctor of Emotional
Breakdown — he told that Mayor to get in that car without
his pubic hair and drive to Kill get to Las Vegas so the
oldfashioned jewish communists
wouldn't get their idealistic radio program on the air in time to
make everybody cry in the desert for the Indian Serpent
to come
back from the Oklahoma mound where he hid with his
15,000,000 visionary original Redskin patriot-wives and
warriors — they made up one big mystic serpent with its
tail-a-mouth like a lost Tibet
MURDERED AND DRIVEN FROM THE EARTH BY US
JEWISH GOYIM who spend fifty billion things a year —
things things! — to make the things-machinery that's

turned the worlds of human consciousness into a thing of
    War
wherever and whoever is plugged in by real filaments or wireless
    or whatever magic wordy-synapse to the money-center of
    the mind
whose Eye is hidden somewhere behind All mass media — what
    makes reporters fear their secret dreamy news — behind the
    Presidential mike & all its starry bunting, front for some
    mad BILLIONAIRES
who own United Fruits & Standard Oil and Hearst The Press
    and Texas NBC and someone owns the Radios owns vast
    Spheres of Air — Subliminal Billionaire got
State Legislatures filled with Capital Punishment Fiends because
    nobody's been in love on US soil long enough to realize
    We who pay the Public Hangman make State Murder thru
    Alien Gas who cause any form of hate-doom hanging
do that in public everybody agreed by the neck suffering utmost
    pangs Each citizen himself unloved suicides him, because
    there's no beloved, now in America for All in the gas
    chamber the whole California Legislature
screaming because its Death here — we're so hopeless — The
    Soul of America died with ugly Chessman — strange saintly
    average madman driven to think for his own killers, in his
    pants and shirt with human haircut, said NO to — like a
    Cosmic NO — from the One Mouth of America speaking
    life or death — looked in the eye by America —
Ah what a cold monster OneEye he must've saw thru the Star
    Spangled Banner & Hollywood with ugly smile forbidden
    movie & old heartless Ike in the White House officially
    allowing Chatterley attacked by Fed Lawyers —
vast Customs agencies searching books — who Advises what
    book where — who invented what's dirty? The Pope?

Baruch? — tender Genet burned by middleaged vice Officers

sent out by The Automatic Sourface mongers whatever bad news he can high up from imaginary Empires name Scripps-Howard — just more drear opinions — Damn that *World Telegram* was Glad Henry Miller's depression Cancerbook not read to sad eyeglass Joe messenger to Grocer

in Manhattan, or candystore emperor Hirsh Silverman in Bayonne, dreaming of telling the *Truth*, but his Karma is selling jellybeans & being kind,

The Customs police denyd him his Burroughs they defecated on de Sade, they jack'd off, and tortured his copy of Sodom with Nitric Acid in a backroom furnace house at Treasury Bureau, pouring Fire on the soul of Rochester,

Warlocks, Black magicians burning and cursing the Love-Books, Jack be damned, casting spells from the shores of America on the inland cities, lacklove-curses on our Eyes which read genital poetry —

O deserts of deprivation for some high school'd gang, lone Cleveland that delayed its books of Awe, Chicago struggling to read its magazines, police and papers yapping over grimy gossip skyscraped from some sulphurous yellow cloud drift in from archtank hot factories make nebulous explosives near Detroit — smudge got on Corso's Rosy Page —

US Postmaster, first class sexfiend his disguise told everyone to open letters stop the photographic fucks & verbal suckeries & lickings of the asshole by tongues meant but for poison glue on envelopes Report this privileged communication to Yours Truly We The National Police — We serve you once a day — you humanical meat creephood —

and yearly the national furnace burned much book, 2,000,000 pieces mail, one decade unread propaganda from Vietnam

     & Chinese mag harangues, Engelian

dialectics handmade in Gobi for proud export to top hat & tails
     Old Bones in his penthouse on a skyscraper in Manhattan,
     laconic on two phones that rang thru the nets of money
     over earth, as he barked his orders to Formosa for more
     spies, abhorred all Cuba sugar from concourse with Stately
     stomachs —

That's when I began vomiting my paranoia when Old National
     Skullface the invisible sixheaded billionaire began brain-
     washing my stomach with strange feelers in the *Journal
     American* — the penis of billionaires depositing professional
     semen in my ear, Fulton Lewis *coming* with strychnine
     jizzum in his voice making an evil suggestion that entered
     my mouth

while I was sitting there gaping in wild dubiety & astound on
     my peaceful couch, he said to all the taxidrivers and
     schoolteachers in brokendown old Blakean America

that Julius and Ethyl Rosenberg smelled bad & shd die, he sent
     to kill them with personal electricity, his power station is
     the spirit of generation leaving him thru his asshole by
     Error, that very electric entered Ethyl's eye

and his tongue is the prick of a devil he don't even know, a
     magic capitalist ghosting it on the lam after the Everett
     Massacre — fucks a Newscaster in the mouth every time he
     gets on the Microphone —

and those ghost jizzums started my stomach trouble with capital
     punishment, Ike chose to make an Artificial Death for them
     poor spies — if they were spying on me? who cares? — Ike
     disturbed the balance of the cosmos by his stroke-head
     deathshake, " NO "

It was a big electrocution in every paper and mass media,
     Television was a baby crawling toward that deathchamber

Later quiz shows prepared the way for **egghead omelette, I was**
rotten, I was the egghead that spoiled the last supper, they
made me vomit more — whole programs of halfeaten
comedians sliming out my Newark Labour Leaders' assholes
They used to wash them in the 30's with **Young Politics Ideas,**
I was too young to smell anything but my own secret mind,
I didn't even know assholes basic to **Modern Democracy —**
What can we teach our negros now?
That they are Negros, that I am thy Jew & thou my white Goy
& him Chinese? — They think they're Arab Macrocosms
now!
My uncle thinks his Truthcloud's Jewish — thinks his Name is
Nose-smell-Newark 5 decades — & that's all except there's
Gentile Images of mirrory vast Universe —
and Chinese Microcosms too, a race of spade microcosms apart,
like jewish truth clouds & Goyisha Nameless Vasts
But I am the Intolerant One Gasbag from the Morgue & Void,
Garbler of all Conceptions that myope my eye & is Uncle
Sam asleep in the Funeral Home — ?
Bad magic, scram, hide in J. E. Hoover's bathingsuit. Make his
pants fall in the ocean, near Miami —
Gangster CRASH! America will be forgotten, the identity files
of the FBI slipt into the void-crack, the fingerprints
unwhorled — no track where He came from —
Man left no address, not even hair, just disappeared & Forgot
his big wallstreet on Earth — Uncle I hate the FBI it's all
a big dreamy skyscraper somewhere over the Mutual
Network — I don't even know who they are — like the
Nameless —

Halooo I am coming end of my Presidency — Everybody's
fired — I am a hopeless whitehaired congressman — I lost

my last election — landslide for **Reader's Digest** — not even humans —

Nobody home in town — just offices with many jangling telephones & automatic switchboards keep the message — typewriters return yr calls oft, Yakkata yak & tinbellring — THE POLICE ARE AT THE DOOR —

What are you doing eccentric in this solitary office? a mad vagrant Creep Truthcloud sans identity card — It's Paterson allright — anyway the people disappeared — downtown Fabian Bldg. branch office for The Chamber of Commerce runs the streetlights

all thru dark winter rain by univac piped from Washington Lobby — they've abolished the streets from the universe — just keep control of

the lights — in case of ectoplasm trafficking thru dead Market — where the Chinese restaurant usta play Muzak in the early century — soft green rugs & pastel walls — perfumèd tea —

Goodby, said the metal Announcer in doors of The Chamber of Commerce — we're merging with NAM forever — and the NAM has no door but's sealed copper 10 foot vault under the Federal Reserve Bldg —

Six billionaires that control America are playing Scrabble with antique Tarot — they've just unearthed another Pyramid — in the bombproof Cellar at Fort Knox

Not even the FBI knows who — They give orders to J. E. Hoover thru the metal phonegirl at the Robot Transmitter on top of RCA — you

can see new Fortune officers look like spies from 20 floors below with their eyeglasses & gold skulls — silver teeth flashing up the shit-mouthed grin — weeping in their martinis! There is no secret to the success of the

Six Billionaires that own all Time since the Gnostic Revolt in
    Aegypto — they built the Sphinx to confuse my sex life,
    Who Fuckd the Void?
Why are they starting that war all over again in Laos over
    Neutral Mind? Is the United States CIA army Legions
    overthrowing somebody like Angelica Balibanoff?
Six thousand movietheaters, 100,000,000 television sets, a billion
    radios, wires and wireless crisscrossing hemispheres,
    semaphore lights and morse, all telephones ringing at once
    connect every mind by its ears to one vast consciousness
    This Time Apocalypse — everybody waiting for one mind
    to break thru —
Man-prophet with two eyes Dare all creation with his dying
    tongue & say I AM — Messiah swallow back his death into
    his stomach, gaze thru great pupils of his Bodies' eyes
and look in each Eye man, the eyeglassed fearful byriad-look
    that might be Godeyes see thru Death — that now are clark
    & ego reading manlaw — write newsbroadcasts to cover
    with Fears their
own Messiah that must come when all of us conscious —
    Breakthru to all other Consciousness to say the Word I
    Am as spoken by a certain God — Millennia knew and
    waited till this one Century —

Now all sentience broods and listens — contemplative & hair full
    of rain for 15 years inside New York — what millions know
    and hark to hear, & death will tell, but —
many strange magicians in buildings listening inside their own
    heads — or clouds over Manhattan Bridge — or strained
    thru music messages to — I Am from the central One!
    Come
blow the Cosmic Horn to waken every Tiglon & Clown sentience

throughout the vasting circus — in the Name of God pick
up the telephone call Networks announcing Suchness
That —

I Am mutter a million old Gods in their beards, that had been
sleeping at evening radios — cackling in their Larynx —
Talking to myself again

said the Messiah turning a dial to remember his last broadcast —
I scare myself, I eat my hand, I swallow my own head,
I stink in the inevitable bathroom of death this Being
requires — O Widen the Area of Consciousness! O

set my Throne in Space, I rise to sit in the midst of the Starry
Visible! — Calling All Beings! in dirt from the ant to the
most frightened Prophet that ever clomb tower to vision
planets

crowded in one vast space ship toward Andromeda — That all
lone soul in Iowa or Hark-land join the Lone, set forth, walk
naked like a Hebrew king, enter the human cities and speak
free,

at last the Man-God come that hears all Phantasy behind the
matter-babble in his ear, and walks out of his Cosmic Dream
into the cosmic street

open mouth to the First Consciousness — God's woke up now,
you Seraphim, call men with trumpet microphone &
telegraph, hail every sleepwalker with Holy Name,

Life is waving, the cosmos is sending a message to itself, its
image is reproduced endlessly over TV

over the radio the babble of Hitler's and Claudette Colbert's
voices got mixed up in the bathroom radiator

Hello hello are you the Telephone the Operator's singing we are
the daughters of the universe

get everybody on the line at once plug in all being ears by

laudspeaker, newspeak, secret message,

handwritten electronic impulse travelling along rays electric
spiderweb

magnetisms shuddering on one note We We We, mustached disc
jockeys trembling in mantric excitement, flowery patterns
bursting over the broken couch,

drapes falling to the floor in St.-Jean Perse's penthouse,
Portugal's water is running in all the faucets on the SS
Santa Rosa,

chopping machines descend on the pre-dawn tabloid, the wire
services are hysterical and send too much message,

they're waiting to bam out the Armageddon, millions of rats
reported in China, smoke billows out New York's hospital
furnace smokestack,

I am writing millions of letters a year, I correspond with hopeful
messengers in Detroit, I am taking drugs

and leap at my postman for more correspondence, Man is leaving
the earth in a rocket ship,

there is a mutation of the race, we are no longer human beings,
we are one being, we are being connected to itself,

it makes me crosseyed to think how, the mass media assemble
themselves like congolese Ants for a purpose

in the massive clay mound an undiscovered huge Queen is born,
Africa wakes to redeem the old Cosmos,

I am masturbating in my bed, I dreamed a new Stranger touched
my heart with his eye,

he hides in a sidestreet loft in Hoboken, the heavens have
covered East Second Street with Snow,

all day I walk in the wilderness over white carpets of City, we
are redeeming ourself, I am born,

the Messiah woke in the Universe, I announce the New Nation,
in every mind, take power over the dead creation,

I am naked in New York, a star breaks thru the blue skull of the
sky out the window,

I seize the tablets of the Law, the spectral Buddha and the spectral
Christ turn to a stick of shit in the void, a fearful Idea,

I take the crown of the Idea and place it on my head, and sit a
King beside the reptile Devas of my Karma —

Eye in every forehead sleeping waxy & the light gone inward —
to dream of fearful Jaweh or the Atom Bomb —

All these eternal spirits to be wakened, all these bodies touched
and healed, all these lacklove

suffering the Hate, dumbed under rainbows of Creation, O Man
the means of Heaven are at hand, thy rocks & my rocks are
nothing,

the identity of the Moon is the identity of the flower-thief, I
and the Police are one in revolutionary Numbness!

Yawk, Mercy The Octopus, it's IT cometh over the Void &
makes whistle its lonemouthed Flute You-me forever —

Stop Arguing, Cosmos, I give up so I be, I receive a happy letter
from Ray Bremser exiled from home in New Jersey jail —

Clocks are abuilding for a thousand years, ticking behind metal-
loidesque electronico-clankered industries smokeless in silent
mind city —

Dawn of the Ages! Man thy Alarm rings thru sweet myriad
mornings in every desperate-carred street! Saints wait in
each metropolis

for Message to Assassinate the old idea, that 20,000 yr old
eye-god Man thought was Being Secret mystery,

unbearable Judge above, God alien handless tongueless to poor
man, who'll scream for mercy on his deathbed — Oh I saw
that black

Octopus Death, with supernatural antennae spikes raying Awful

waves at my consciousness, huge blind Ball invisible behind
  the rooms in the universe — a not-a-man — a no-one
  — Nobodaddy —
Omnipotent Telepath more visionary than my own Prophetics &
  Memories — Reptile-sentient shimmer-feel-hole Here,
Dense Soullessness wiser than Time, the Eater-Darkness hungry
  for All — but must wait till I leave my body to enter that
One Mind nebula to my recollection — Implacable, my soul
  dared not die,
Shrank back from the leprous door-mind in its breast, touch Him
  and the hand's destroyed,
Death God in the End, before the Timeworld of creation — I
  mean some kind of monster from another dimension is
  eating Beings of our own Cosmos —
I saw him try to make me leave my corpse-illusion Allen, myth
  movie world come to celluloid-end,
I screamed seeing myself in reels of death my consciousness a
  cinematic toy played once in faded attick by man-already-
  forgotten
His orphan starhood inked from Space, the movie industry itself
  blot up its History & all wracked myriad Epics, Space wiped
  itself out,
lost in a wall-crack dream itself had once disappearing — maybe
  trailing endless comet-long trackless thru what unwonted
  dimensions it keeps dreaming existence can die inside of —
  vanish this Cosmos of Stars I am turning to bones in —
That much illusion, and what's visions but visions, and these
  words filled Methedrine — I have a backache & 2 telegrams
  come midnight from messengers that cry to plug in the

Electrode Ear to
my skull downstreet, & hear what they got to say, big lives like
trees of Cancer in Bronx & Long Island — Telephones
connect the voids island blissy darkness scattered in many
manmind —

New York City Winter 1961

THIS FORM OF LIFE NEEDS SEX

I will have to accept women
                    if I want to continue the race,
              kiss breasts, accept
              strange hairy lips behind
                              buttocks,
Look in questioning womanly eyes
                    answer soft cheeks,
bury my loins in the hang of pearplum
                    fat tissue
                         I had abhorred
before I give godspasm Babe leap
         forward thru death —
Between me and oblivion an unknown
                    woman stands;
Not the Muse but living meat-phantom,
a mystery scary as my fanged god
              sinking its foot in its gullet &
vomiting its own image out of its ass
— This woman Futurity I am pledge to
                    born not to die,
but issue my own cockbrain replica Me-Hood
         again — For fear of the Blot?
Face of Death, my Female, as I'm sainted
              to my very bone,
I'm fated to find me a maiden for
                    ignorant Fuckery —
flapping my belly & smeared with Saliva
         shamed face flesh & wet,

— have long droopy conversations
      in Cosmical Duty boudoirs,
          maybe bored?
Or excited New Prospect, discuss
    her, Futurity, my Wife
        My Mother, Death, My only
            hope, my very Resurrection
Woman
        herself, why have I feared
         to be joined true
    embraced beneath the Panties of Forever
in with the one hole that repelled me 1937 on?
— Pulled down my pants on the porch showing
    my behind to cars passing in rain —
& She be interested, this contact
              with Silly new Male
    that's sucked my loveman's cock
in Adoration & sheer beggary romance-awe
    gulp-choke Hope of Life come
and buggered myself innumerably boy-yangs
      gloamed inward so my solar plexus
      feel godhead in me like an open door —

Now that's changed my decades body old
tho admiring male thighs at my brow,
    hard love pulsing thru my ears,
      stern buttocks upraised
          for my masterful Rape
    that were meant for a private shit
        if the Army were All —
But no more answer to life
        than the muscular statue

I felt up its marbles
envying Beauty's immortality in the
                museum of Yore —
You can fuck a statue but you cant
        have children
You can joy man to man but the Sperm
            comes back in a trickle at dawn
        in a toilet on the 45th Floor —
& Can't make continuous mystery out of that
        finished performance
                        & ghastly thrill
    that ends as began,
                    stupid reptile squeak
        denied life by Fairy Creator
            become Imaginary
        because he decided not to incarnate
            opposite — Old Spook
who didn't want to be a baby & die,
        didn't want to shit and scream
            exposed to bombardment on a
                    Chinese RR track
and grow up to pass his spasm on
        the other half of the Universe —
Like a homosexual capitalist afraid of
                    the masses —
and that's my situation, Folks —

4/12/61

SUNSET *S.S. AZEMOUR*

As orange dusk-light falls on an old idea
I gaze thru my hand on the page
sensing outward the intercoiled weird being I am in
and seek a head of that — Seraphim
advance in lightening flash through aether storm
Messengers arrive horned bearded from Magnetic spheres
disappearing radios receive aged galaxies
Immensity wheels mirrored in every direction
Announcement swifting from Invisible to Invisible
Eternity-dragon's tail lost to the eye
Strange death, forgotten births, voices calling in the past
" I was " that greets " I am " that writes now " I will be "
Armies marching over and over the old battlefield —
What powers sit in their domed tents and decree Eternal Victory?
I sit at my desk and scribe the endless message from myself to my
       own hand

Marseilles-Tanger 1961

SEABATTLE OF SALAMIS TOOK PLACE
OFF PERAMA

If it weren't for you Mr Jukebox with yr aluminum belly
    roaring & thirty teeth eating dirty drx.
yr eyes starred round the world, purple diamonds & white
    brain revolving black disks
in every bar from Yokamama to Pyraeus winking & beaming
    Saturday Nite
what silence harbor Sabbath dark instead of boys screaming and
    dancing wherever I go —
Hail Jukebox of Perama with attendant minstrel juvenile whores
on illuminated porches where kids leap to noise bouncing over
    black oceantide,
leaning into azure neon with sexy steps, delicious idiot smile and
    young teeth, flowers in ears,
Negro voices scream back 1000 years striped pants pink shirts
    patent leather shoes on their lean dog feet
exaggerated sneakers green pullovers, long hair, hips & eyes!
They're jumping & joying this minute over the bones of Persian
    sailors —
Echoes of Harlem in Athens! Hail to your weeping eyes New
    York!
Hail to the noise wherever the jukebox is on TOO LOUD,
The Muses are loose in the world again with their big black
    voice bazookey blues,
Muses with bongo guitars electric flutes on microphones Cha
    Cha Cha
Feeling happy in Havana Mambo moving delicate London new
    Lyre in Liverpool
Tin Clarinet prophesying in Delphos, Crete jumping again!

Panyotis dancing alone stepped drunk from a krater, Yorgis
slapping his heels & kicking Cerberus' heads off!
Doobie Doobie reigns forever on the shores! One drachma for
Black Jack, one drachma brings Aharisti again, Na-ti-the-
Ma-Fez,
Open the Door Richard, I'm Casting a Spell on You, Apocalypse
Rock, End of History Rag!

1961

GALILEE SHORE

With the blue-dark dome old-starred at night, green boat-lights
    purring over water,
a faraway necklace of cliff-top Syrian electrics,
bells ashore, music from a juke-box trumpeted,
shadow of death against my left breast prest
— cigarette, match-flare, skull wetting its lips —

Fisherman-nets over wood walls, light wind in dead willow branch
on a grassy bank — the saxophone relaxed and brutal, silver
    horns echo —
Was there a man named Solomon? Peter walked here? Christ
    on this sweet water?
Blessings on thee Peacemaker!

                        English spoken
on the street bearded Jews' sandals & Arab white head cloth —
the silence between Hebrew and Arabic —
the thrill of the first Hashish in a holy land —
Over hill down the valley in a blue bus, past Cana no weddings —
I have no name I wander in a nameless countryside —
young boys all at the movies seeing a great Western —
art gallery closed, pipe razor & tobacco on the floor.

To touch the beard of Martin Buber
to watch a skull faced Gershom Scholem lace his shoes
to pronounce Capernaum's name & see stone doors of a tomb
to be meek, alone, beside a big dark lake at night —
to pass thru Nazareth dusty afternoon, and smell the urine down
    near Mary's well
to watch the orange moon peep over Syria, weird promise —

to wait beside Galilee — night with Orion, lightning, negro voices,
    Burger's Disease, a glass of lemon tea — feel my left hand
    on my shaved chin —
all you have to do is suffer the metaphysical pain of dying.
Art is just a shadow, like cows or tea —
keep the future open, make no dates it's all here
with moonrise and soft music on phonograph memory —
Just think how amazing! someone getting up and walking on
    the water.

Tiberias 10/61

STOTRAS TO KALI DESTROYER OF ILLUSIONS

O Statue of Liberty Spouse of Europa Destroyer of Past Present
    Future

They who recite this Anthem issuing from empty skulls the stars
    & stripes

certainly makes a noise on the radio beauteous with the twilight

should one skinny Peruvian only spell your name right O thou
    who

hast formidable eyebrows of spiritual money & beareth United
    Nations in your hair

such Peruvian becomes higher Jaweh charming countless
    moviestars with disappearing eyes

O republic female mouth from which two politics trickle they
    who recite

the name thy 28th star OMAHA subjugate hungry ghost-hoards
    ascreech under Gold Reserve

O fortress America Guardian Blueprint who in thy nether right
    hand hangs a bathroom

in thy nether left the corpse of Edgar Poe in front right hand
    hanging the skull

of Roosevelt with grey eyeballs & left hand George Washington
    his tongue hanging out like a fish

Your huge goddess eye looming over his severed head your
    bottomless throat open

with great machinery roars inside teeth made of white radios &
    mountainous red tongue

licking vast bubbles of atomic gum left eye rolled to grey
    heavens above Dewline

right eye staring into magic engine wheels hissing with rail-
    road steam

arm after arm snaking into place in aether battleships dangling
    from one hand to another

the black corpse Thelonious Monk the flayed skin of Gertrude
    Stein held down

fluttering over the gaping Yoni, hands reaching out to honk all
    the horns of Broadway

William Randolph Hearst's bones circled in mystic ring on third
    toe & breast hung

with newspapers shining with Earl Browder's cancer the 1964
    Elections flapping in her left

nostril if you sneeze you'll destroy the western hemisphere right
    Vajra hand

playing mahjong with her astrolabes it keeps her mind occupied
    especially with rhythmic

breathing exercises & interpretive dancing one foot goddesslike
    on the corpse of Uncle Sam

Top hand bearing the Telephone nobody's on the other end she's
    talking to herself

because when the ear gets disconnected from the brain you still
    hear noise

but who remembers what it means somebody else will pay the
    bill as fast as it takes

for vultures to clean up a corpse at Tower of Silence That will
    be five minutes and

extra charges if you go on talking the eleventh hand presenting
    an electric chair

twelfth hand in the mudra of Foreign Aid and thirteenth palm
    closed in sign of Disarmament

O Freedom with gaping mouth full of Cops whose throat is
  adorned with skulls of Rosenbergs
whose breasts spurt Jazz into the robot faces of thy worshippers
  grant that recitation
of this Hymn will bring them abiding protection money & dance
  in White House
for even a dope sees Eternity who meditates on thee raimented
  with Space crosseyed
creatrix of Modernity whose waist is beauteous with a belt of
  numberless Indian scalps
mixed with negro teeth Who on the breast of James Dean in the
  vast bedroom of Forest Lawn
Cemetery enjoyest the great Passion of Jesus Christ or seated on
  the boneyard ground
strewn with the flesh of Lumumba haunted by the female shoes
  of Kruschev & Stevenson's long red tongue
enjoyest the worship of spies & endless devotions intoned by
  mustached radio announcers
If by night thy devotee naked with long weird hair sit in the
  park & recite this Hymn
while his full breasted girl fills his lap with provincial kisses and
  meditates on Thee
Such such a one dwells in the land the supreme politician &
  knows Thy mystery
O Wife of China should thy patriot recite thy anthem & China's
  cut-up & mixed together
with that of Russia Thy elephant-headed infant mighty in all
  future worlds
& meditate one year with knowledge of thy mystic copulation
  with China this next age
Then such knower will delight in secret weapon official
  Intelligence kodaked in his telegraphic brain

Home of the Brave thou gavest birth to the Steel Age before the
    Hydrogen Age the
Cobalt Age earning power over entire planets all futurity Male-
    female spouse of the solar system
Ah me why then shall I not prophesy glorious truths for Thee
    Ah me folks worship many other
countries beside you they are brainwashed but I of my own
    uncontrollable lust for you
lay my hands on your Independence enter your very Constitution
    my head absorbed in the lips of your
Bill of Rights O Liberty whose bliss is union with each individual
    citizen intercourse
Alaskan Oklahoman New Jerseyesque dreaming of embraces even
    Indonesian Vietnamese & those Congolese
O Liberty Imagewife of Mankind of thy Mercy show thy favor
    toward each me everywhere helpless
before thy manifest Destiny by grace may I never be reborn
    American I and all I's
neither Russian Peruvian nor Chinese Jew never again reincarn-
    ate outside Thee Mother
Democracy O Formless One take me beyond Images & reproduc-
    tions spouse beyond disunion
absorbed in my own non-Duality which art Thou.

He O mother American Democracy who in the cremation ground
    of nations with dishevelled hair in sweat of intensity
    meditates on thee
And makes over his pubic hair to thee in poetry or electrical
    engineering he alone knows thy Cosmic You-Me.
O America whoever on Tuesday at midnite utters This My
    Country Tis of Thee in the basement men's room
of the Empire State Building becomes a Poet Lord of Earth and

goes mounted on Elephants
to conquer Maya the Cold War whoever recites this my country
     tis of thee with the least halfhearted
conviction he becomes himself Big Business & Giant Unions
     flowing with production and is after
death father of his country which is the Universe itself and will
     at night in union with Thee
O mother with eyes of delightful movies enter at last into
     amorous play united with all Presidents of US.

Bombay 1962

DESCRIBE: THE RAIN ON DASASWAMEDH

Kali Ma tottering up steps to shelter tin roof, feeling her way to
   curb, around bicycle & leper seated on her way — to piss on
   a broom

left by the Stone Cutters who last night were shaking the street
   with Boom! of Stone blocks unloaded from truck

Forcing the blindman in his grey rags to retreat from his spot in
   the middle of the road where he sleeps & shakes under his
   blanket

Jai Ram all night telling his beads or sex on a burlap carpet

Past which cows donkeys dogs camels elephants marriage proces-
   sions drummers tourists lepers and bathing devotees

step to the whine of serpent-pipes & roar of car motors around
   his black ears —

Today on a balcony in shorts leaning on iron rail I watched the
   leper who sat hidden behind a bicycle

emerge dragging his buttocks on the grey rainy ground by the
   glove-bandaged stumps of hands,

one foot chopped off below knee, round stump-knob wrapped
   with black rubber

pushing a tin can shiny size of his head with left hand (from
   which only a thumb emerged from leprous swathings)

beside him, lifting it with both ragbound palms down the curb
   into the puddled road,

balancing his body down next to the can & crawling forward
   on his behind

trailing a heavy rag for seat, and leaving a path thru the street
   wavering

like the Snail's slime track — imprint of his crawl on the muddy
   asphalt market entrance — stopping

to drag his can along stubbornly konking on the paved surface
   near the water pump —

Where a turban'd workman stared at him moving along — his
   back humped with rags —

and inquired why didn't he put his can to wash in the pump
   altarplace — and why go that way when free rice

Came from the alley back there by the river — As the leper
   looked up & rested, conversing curiously, can by his side
   approaching a puddle.

Kali had pissed standing up & then felt her way back to the
   Shop Steps on thin brown legs

her hands in the air — feeling with feet for her rag pile on the
   stone steps' wetness —

as a cow busied its mouth chewing her rags left wet on the
   ground for five minutes digesting

Till the comb-&-hair-oil-booth keeper woke & chased her away
   with a stick

Because a dog barked at a madman with dirty wild black hair
   who rag round his midriff & water pot in hand

Stopped in midstreet turned round & gazed up at the balconies,
   windows, shops and city stagery filled with glum activity

Shrugged & said *Jai Shankar!* to the imaginary audience of Me's,

While a white robed Baul Singer carrying his one stringed dried
   pumpkin Guitar

Sat down near the cigarette stand and surveyed his new scene,
   just arrived in the Holy City of Benares.

February 1963

DEATH NEWS

*Visit to W.C.W. circa 1957, poets Kerouac Corso Orlovsky
on sofa in living room inquired wise words, stricken Williams
pointed thru window curtained on Main Street, " There's a lot
of bastards out there!"*

Walking at night on asphalt campus
road by the German Instructor with Glasses
W.C. Williams is dead he said in accent
under the trees in Benares; I stopped and asked
Williams is Dead? Enthusiastic and wide-eyed
under the Big Dipper. Stood on the Porch
of the International House Annex bungalow
insects buzzing round the electric light
reading the Medical obituary in *Time.*
" out among the sparrows behind the shutters "
Williams is in the Big Dipper. He isn't dead
as the many pages of words arranged thrill
with his intonations the mouths of meek kids
becoming subtle even in Bengal. Thus
there's a life moving out of his pages; Blake
also " alive " thru his experienced machines.
Were his last words anything Black out there
in the carpeted bedroom of the gabled wood house
in Rutherford? Wonder what he said,
or was there anything left in realms of speech
after the stroke & brain-thrill doom entered
his thoughts? If I pray to his soul in Bardo Thodol
he may hear the unexpected vibration of foreign mercy.
Quietly unknown for three weeks; now I saw Passaic
and Ganges one, consenting his devotion,

because he walked on the steeley bank & prayed
to a Goddess in the river, that he only invented,
another Ganga-Ma. Riding on the old
rusty Holland submarine on the ground floor
Paterson Museum instead of a celestial crockodile.
Mourn O Ye Angels of the Left Wing! that the poet
of the streets is a skeleton under the pavement now
and there's no other old soul so kind and meek
and feminine jawed and him-eyed can see you
What you wanted to be among the bastards out there.

March 20, 1963

VULTURE PEAK: *Gridhakuta Hill*

I've got to get out of the sun
mouth dry and red towel wrapped
            round my head
walking up crying singing *ah sunflower*
Where the traveller's journey
closed my eyes *is done* in the
             black hole there
              sweet rest far far away
up the stone climb past where
Bimbisara left his armies
got down off his elephant
and walked up to meet
Napoleon Buddha pacing
        back and forth on the platform
        of red brick on the jut rock crag
Staring out Lidded-eyed beneath
the burning white sunlight
down on Rajgir kingdom below
      ants wheels within wheels of empire
      houses carts streets messengers
         wells and water flowing
           into past-future simultaneous
         kingdoms here gone on Jupiter
distant X-ray twinkle of the eye
myriad brick cities on earth and under
New York Chicago Palenque Jerusalem
         Delphos Macchu Picchu Acco
          Herculaneum Rajagriha
here all windy with the tweetle
        of birds and blue rocks

leaning into the blue sky —
Vulture Peak desolate bricks
flies on the knee hot shadows
raven-screetch and wind blast
over the hills from desert plains
south toward Bodh Gaya —
All the noise I made with my mouth
singing on the path up, Gary
Thinking all the *pale youths* and
virgins shrouded with snow
chanting Om Shantih all over the world
and who but *Peter du Peru*
walking the streets of San Francisco
arrived in my mind on Vulture Peak
Then turned round and around on my heels
singing and plucking out my eyes
ears tongue nose and balls as I whirled
longer and longer the mountains stretched
swiftly flying in circles
the hills undulating and roads speeding
around me in the valley
Till when I stopped the earth
moved in my eyeballs
green bulge slowly
and stopped
*   *   *

My thirst in my cheeks and tongue
back throat drives me home.

April 18, 1963

PATNA-BENARES EXPRESS

Whatever it may be whoever it may be
The bloody man all singing all just
However he die
He rode on railroad cars
He woke at dawn, in the white light of a new universe
He couldn't do any different
He the skeleton with eyes
raised himself up from a wooden bench
felt different looking at the fields and palm trees
no money in the bank of dust
no nation but inexpressible grey clouds before sunrise
lost his identity cards in his wallet
in the bald rickshaw by the Maidan in dry Patna
Later stared hopeless waking from drunken sleep
dry mouthed in the RR Station
among sleeping shoeshine men in loincloth on the dirty
     concrete
Too many bodies thronging these cities now

5/63

LAST NIGHT IN CALCUTTA

Still night. The old clock Ticks,
half past two. A ringing of crickets
awake in the ceiling. The gate is locked
on the street outside — sleepers, mustaches,
nakedness, but no desire. A few mosquitos
waken the itch, the fan turns slowly —
a car thunders along the black asphalt,
a bull snorts, something is expected —
Time sits solid in the four yellow walls.
No one is here, emptiness filled with train
whistles & dog barks, answered a block away.
Pushkin sits on the bookshelf, Shakespeare's
complete works as well as Blake's unread —
O Spirit of Poetry, no use calling on you
babbling in this emptiness furnished with beds
under the bright oval mirror — perfect
night for sleepers to dissolve in tranquil
blackness, and rest there eight hours
— Waking to stained fingers, bitter mouth
and lung gripped by cigarette hunger,
what to do with this big toe, this arm
this eye in the starving skeleton-filled
sore horse tramcar-heated Calcutta in
Eternity — sweating and teeth rotted away —
Rilke at least could dream about lovers,
the old breast excitement and trembling belly,
is that it? And the vast starry space —
If the brain changes matter breathes
fearfully back on man — But now

the great crash of buildings and planets
breaks thru the walls of language and drowns
me under its Ganges heaviness forever.
No escape but thru Bangkok and New York death.
Skin is sufficient to be skin, that's all
it ever could be, tho screams of pain in the kidney
make it sick of itself, a wavy dream
dying to finish its all too famous misery
— Leave immortality for another to suffer like a fool,
not get stuck in the corner of the universe
sticking morphine in the arm and eating meat.

5/22/63

THE CHANGE: Kyoto-Tokyo Express

I

Black Magicians

Come home : the pink meat image
    black yellow image with
    ten fingers and two eyes
is gigantic already : the black
    curly pubic hair, the
    blind hollow stomach.
the silent soft open vagina
    rare womb of new birth
cock lone and happy to be home
                again
touched by hands by mouths,
    by hairy lips —

Close the portals of the festival?

Open the portals to what Is,
The mattress covered with sheets,
    soft pillows of skin,
long soft hair and delicate
    palms along the buttocks
    timidly touching,
waiting for a sign, a throb
    softness of balls, rough
    nipples alone in the dark
    met by a weird finger;
Tears alright, and laughter
    alright
I am that I am —

Closed off from this
The schemes begin, roulette,
brainwaves, bony dice,
Stroboscope motorcycles
Stereoscopic Scaly
Serpents winding thru
cloud spaces of
what is not —
" plunging on a moth, a butterfly, a
pismire, a —"

II

Shit ! Intestines boiling in sand fire
creep yellow brain cold sweat
earth unbalanced vomit thru
tears, snot ganglia buzzing
the Electric Snake rising hypnotic
shuffling metal-eyed coils
whirling rings within wheels
from asshole up the spine
Acid in the throat the chest
a knot trembling Swallow back
the black furry ball of the great
Fear

Oh !

The serpent in my bed pitiful
crawling unwanted babes of
snake covered with veins and pores
breathing heavy frightened love
metallic Bethlehem out the window

the lost, the lost hungry
ghosts here alive trapped
in carpet rooms   How can I
be sent to Hell
with my skin and blood

Oh I remember myself so

Gasping, staring at dawn over
lower Manhattan   the bridges
covered with rust, the slime
in my mouth & ass, sucking
his cock like a baby crying Fuck
me in my asshole   Make love
to this rotten slave   Give me the
power to whip & eat your heart
I own your belly & your eyes
I speak thru your screaming
mouth Black Mantra Fuck you
Fuck me Mother Brother Friend
old white haired creep shuddering in
the toilet slum bath floorboards —

Oh how wounded, how wounded, I
murder the beautiful chinese women

It will come on the railroad, beneath
the wheels, in drunken hate screaming
thru the skinny machine gun, it will
come out of the mouth of the pilot,
the dry lipped diplomat, the hairy
teacher will come out of me

again shitting the meat out of
my ears on my cancer deathbed

Oh crying man crying woman
crying guerrilla shopkeeper
crying dysentery boneface on
the urinal street of the Self

Oh Negro beaten in the eye in my
home, oh black magicians
in white skin robes boiling the
stomachs of your children that
you do not die but shudder in
Serpent & worm shape forever
Powerful minds & superhuman
Roar of volcano & rocket in
Your bowels —

Hail to your fierce desire, your
Godly pride, my Heaven's gate
will not be closed until
we enter all —

All human shapes, all
trembling donkeys & apes, all
lovers turned to ghost
all achers on trains &
taxicab bodies sped away
from date with desire, old movies,
all who were refused —

All which was rejected, the
     leper-sexed hungry of
     nazi conventions, hollow
     cheeked arab marxists of Acco
     Crusaders dying of starvation
     in the Holy Land —

Seeking the Great Spirit of the
     Universe in Terrible Godly
     form, O suffering Jews
     burned in the hopeless fire
     O thin Bengali sadhus adoring
     Kali mother hung with
     nightmare skulls O Myself
     under her pounding
     feet !

Yes I am that worm soul under
     the heel of the daemon horses
     I am that man trembling to die
     in vomit & trance in bamboo
     eternities belly ripped by
     red hands of courteous
     chinamen kids — Come sweetly
     now back to my Self as I was —

Allen Ginsberg says this : I am
     a mass of sores and worms
     & baldness & belly & smell
     I am false Name the prey
     of Yamantaka Devourer of

Strange dreams, the prey of
radiation & Police Hells of Law

I am that I am I am the
man & the Adam of hair in
my loins   This is my spirit and
physical shape I inhabit
this Universe Oh weeping
against what is my
own nature for now

Who would deny his own shape's
loveliness in his
dream moment of bed
Who sees his desire to be
horrible instead of Him

Who is, who cringes, perishes,
is reborn a red Screaming
baby? Who cringes before
that meaty shape in
Fear?

In this dream I am the Dreamer
and the Dreamed   I am
that I am Ah but I have
always known

oooh for the hate I have spent
in denying my image & cursing
the breasts of illusion —
Screaming at murderers, trembling

between their legs in fear of the
steel pistols of my mortality —

Come, sweet lonely Spirit, back
to your bodies, come great God
back to your only image, come
to your many eyes & breasts,
come thru thought and
motion up all your
arms the great gesture of
Peace & acceptance Abhya
Mudra Mudra of fearlessness
Mudra of Elephant Calmed &
war-fear ended forever!

The war, the war on Man, the
war on woman, the ghost
assembled armies vanish in
their realms

Chinese American Bardo Thodols
all the seventy hundred hells from
Orleans to Algeria tremble
with tender soldiers weeping

In Russia the young poets rise
to kiss the soul of the revolution
in Viet-nam the body is burned
to show the truth of only the
body in Kremlin & White House
the schemers draw back
weeping from their schemes —

In my train seat I renounce
    my power, so that I do
    live I will die

Over for now the Vomit, cut
    up & pincers in the skull, the
    fear of bones, the grasp
    against man & woman & babe.

Let the dragon of Death
    come forth from his
    picture in the whirling
    white clouds' darkness

And suck dream brains &
    claim these lambs for his
    meat, and let him feed
    and be other than I

Till my turn comes and I
    enter that maw and change
    to a blind rock covered
    with misty ferns that
    I am not all now

but a universe of skin and breath
    & changing thought and
    burning hand & softened
    heart in the old bed of
    my skin   From this single
    birth reborn that I am
    to be so —

My own Identity now nameless
     neither man nor dragon or
     God

but the dreaming Me full
     of physical rays' tender
     red moons in my belly &
     Stars in my eyes circling

And the Sun the Sun the
     Sun my visible father
     making my body visible
     thru my eyes!

7/18/63

WHY IS GOD LOVE, JACK?

Because I lay my
 head on pillows,
Because I weep in the
 tombed studio
Because my heart
 sinks below my navel
because I have an
 old airy belly
 filled with soft
 sighing, and
 remembered breast
 sobs — or
 a hands touch makes
 tender —
Because I get scared —
Because I raise my
 voice singing to
 my beloved self —
Because I do love thee
 my darling, my
 other, my living
 bride
my friend, my old lord
 of soft tender eyes —
Because I am in the
 Power of life & can
 do no more than
 submit to the feeling
 that I am the One
 Lost

Seeking still seeking the
    thrill — delicious
    bliss in the
      heart abdomen loins
        & thighs
Not refusing this
    38 yr. 145 lb. head
    arms & feet of meat
Nor one single Whitmanic
    toenail contemn
nor hair prophetic banish
    to remorseless Hell,
Because wrapped with machinery
I confess my ashamed desire.

MORNING

Ugh ! the planet screams
Doves in rusty cornice-
      castles peer
down on auto crossroads,
    a junkey in white jacket
wavers in yellow light on
     way to a negro in bed
Black smoke flowing on roofs, terrific
     city coughing —
garbage can lids music over
     truck whine on E. 5th St.
Ugh ! I'm awake again —
    dreary day ahead
what to do? — Dull letters
    to be answered
an epistle to M. Duchamp
more me all day the same
clearly

      Q. " Do you want to live or die? "
      A. " I don't know "
   said Julius after 12 years
        State Hospital

Ugh ! cry negros in Harlem
Ugh ! cry License Inspectors, Building
      Inspectors, Police Congressmen,
      Undersecretaries of Defense.
Ugh ! Cries Texas Mississippi !

Ugh! Cries India
Ugh! Cries US
               Well, who knows?

O flowing copious!
    total Freedom! To
Do what? to blap! to
    embarrass! to conjoin
Locomotive blossoms to Leafy
    purple vaginas.
To be dull! ashamed! shot!
    Finished! Flopped!
To say Ugh absolutely mean-
    ingless here
To be a big bore! even to
    myself! Fulla shit!

Paper words! Fblup! Fizzle! Droop!
Shut your big fat mouth!
Go take a flying crap in the
    rain!
Wipe your own ass! Bullshit!
You big creep! Fairy! Dopey
    Daffodil! Stinky Jew!
Mr Professor! Dirty Rat! Fart!

Honey! Darling! Sweetie pie!
Baby! Lovey! Dovey! Dearest!
My own! Buttercup! O Beautiful!
Doll! Snookums! Go fuck
        yourself,
    everybody Ginsberg!

And when you've exhausted
        that, go forward?
Where? kiss my ass!

O Love, my mouth against
     a black policeman's breast.

N.Y. 1963

WAKING IN NEW YORK

I

I place my hand before my beard with awe
and stare thru open-uncurtain window
                    rooftop rose-blue sky thru
                    which small dawn clouds ride
                                rattle against the pane,
            lying on a thick carpet matted floor
                    at last in repose on pillows my knees
                    bent beneath brown himalayan blanket, soft —
            fingers atremble to pen, cramp
                    pressure diddling the page white
                            San Francisco notebook —
And here am on the sixth floor cold
                    March 5th Street old building plaster
                    apartments in ruin, super he drunk
                            with baritone radio AM nose-sex
Oh New York, oh Now our bird
                    flying past glass window Chirp
                    — our life together here
            smoke of tenement chimney pots dawn haze
                    passing thru wind soar Sirs—

How shall we greet Thee this Springtime oh
                                Lords — ?
What gifts give ourselves, what police fear
                    stop searched in late streets
Rockerfeller Frisk No-Knock break down
                    my iron white-painted door?
Where shall I seek Law? in the State
                    in offices of telepath bureaucracy — ?

in my dis-ease, my trembling, my cry
               — ecstatic song to myself
to my police my law my state my
                  many selfs —
Aye, Self is Law and State Police
      Kennedy struck down knew him Self
Oswald, Ruby ourselves
                Till we know our desires Blest
                with babe issue,
                          Resolve, accept
             this self flesh we bear
             in underwear, Bathrobe, smoking cigarette
             up all night — brooding, solitary, set
                  alone, tremorous leg & arm —
                approaching the joy of Alones
                Racked by that, arm laid to rest,
                  head back wide-eyed

Morning, my song to Who listens, to
                myself as I am
To my fellows in this shape that building
                Brooklyn Bridge or Albany name —
                Salute to the self-gods on
                      Pennsylvania Avenue !
May they have mercy on us all,
May be just men not murderers
      Nor the State murder more,
      That all beggars be fed, all
             dying medicined, all loveless
            Tomorrow be loved
                well come & be balm.

3/16/64

II

On the roof cloudy sky fading sun rays
               electric torches atop —
        auto horns — The towers
     with time-hands giant pointing
          late Dusk hour over
             clanky roofs
Tenement streets' brick sagging cornices
        baby white kite fluttering against giant
        insect face-gill Electric Mill
           smokestacked blue & fumes drift up
   Red messages, shining high floors,
        Empire State dotted with tiny windows
        lit, across the blocks
      of spire, steeple, golden topped utility
         building roofs — far like
         pyramids lit in jagged
            desert rocks —

The giant the giant city awake
        in the first warm breath of springtime
Waking voices, babble of Spanish
        street families, radio music
        floating under roofs, longhaired
           announcer sincerity squawking
               cigar voice
        Light zips up phallos stories
        beneath red antennae needling
          thru rooftop chimnies' smog
             black drift thru the blue air —

Bridges curtained by uplit apartment walls,
            one small tower with a light
        on its shoulder below the " moody, water-loving
                                    giants "
The giant stacks burn thick grey
            smoke, Chrysler is lit with green,
down Wall street islands of skyscraper
        black jagged in Sabbath quietness —
Oh fathers, how I am alone in this
            vast human wilderness
Houses uplifted like hives off
            the stone floor of the world —
the city too vast to know, too
            myriad windowed to govern
                from ancient halls —
" O edifice of gas ! " — Sun shafts
        descend on the highest building's
            striped blocktop a red light
                winks buses hiss & rush
                grinding, green lights
                of north bridges,
                    hum roar & Tarzan
                        squeal, whistle
                        swoops, hurrahs !

Is someone dying in all this stone building?
Child poking its black head out of the womb
            like the pupil of an eye?
Am I not breathing here frightened
                    and amazed — ?
Where is my comfort, where's heart-ease,

Where are tears of joy?
Where are the companions? in
            deep homes in Stuyvesant Town
            behind the yellow-window wall?
I fail, book fails, — a lassitude,
                a fear — tho I'm alive
and gaze over the descending — No !
peer in the inky beauty of the roofs.

4/18/64

AFTER YEATS

Now incense fills the air
and delight follows delight,
quiet supper in the carpet room,
music twangling from the Orient to my ear,
old friends at rest on bright mattresses,
old paintings on the walls, old poetry
thought anew, laughing at a mystic toy
statue painted gold, tea on the white table.

April 26, 1964

I AM A VICTIM OF TELEPHONE

When I lay down to sleep dream the Wishing Well it rings
" Have you a new play for the brokendown theater? "
When I write in my notebook poem it rings
" Buster Keaton is under the brooklyn bridge on Frankfurt
    and Pearl . . ."
When I unsheath my skin extend my cock toward someone's
    thighs fat or thin, boy or girl
Tingaling — " Please get him out of jail . . . the police are
    crashing down "
When I lift the soupspoon to my lips, the phone on the floor
    begins purring
" Hello it's me — I'm in the park two broads from Iowa . . .
    nowhere to sleep last night . . . hit 'em in the mouth "
When I muse at smoke crawling over the roof outside my
    street window
purifying Eternity with my eye observation of grey vaporous
    columns in the sky
ring ring " Hello this is Esquire be a dear and finish your
    political commitment manifesto "
When I listen to radio presidents roaring on the convention
    floor
the phone also chimes in " Rush up to Harlem with us and see
    the riots "
Always the telephone linked to all the hearts of the world
    beating at once
crying my husband's gone my boyfriend's busted forever my
    poetry was rejected
won't you come over for money and please won't you write
    me a piece of bullshit

How are you dear can you come to Easthampton we're all
    here bathing in the ocean we're all so lonely
and I lay back on my pallet contemplating $50 phone bill,
    broke, drowsy, anxious, my heart fearful of the fingers
    dialing, the deaths, the singing of telephone bells
ringing at dawn ringing all afternoon ringing up midnight
    ringing now forever.

June 20, 1964

TODAY

O I am happy! O Swami Shivananda — a smile!

O telephone sweet little black being, what many voices and tongues!

Tonight I'll call up Jack tell him Buster Keaton is under the Brooklyn Bridge

by a vast red-brick wall still dead pan alive in red suspenders, portly abdomen.

Today I saw movies, publishers, bookstores, checks — wait, I'm still poor

Poor but happy! I saw politicians we wrote a Noise Law!

A Law to free poetry — Poor Plato! Whoops here comes Fascism! I rode in a taxi!

I rode a bus, ate hot Italian Sausages, Coca Cola, a chiliburger, Cool-Aid I drank —

All day I did things! I took a nap — didn't I dream about lampshade academies and ouch! I am dying?

I stuck a needle in my arm and flooded my head with drowsy bliss . . .

And a hairy bum asked Mr Keaton for money drink! Oh Buster! No answer!

Today I was really amazed! Samuel Beckett had rats eyes and gold round glasses —

I didn't say a word — I had my picture taken and read all thru The NY Times

and Daily News, I read everybody's editorials, I protested in my mind I have the privilege of being

Mad. Today I did everything, I wore a pink shirt in the street, at home in underwear

I marvelled Henry Miller's iron sink, how could he remember

so clearly?

Hypnagogic vision in Brooklyn 50 years ago — just now my
    eyeball

troops marched in square mufti battalion dragging prisoners to —

eyelids lifted I saw a blue devil with fifteen eyes on the wall —
    everything's mine, antique Tibetan Tankas, a siamese cat
    asleep on its side relaxed —

I looked out of the window and saw Tonight, it was dark —
    someone said ooo! in Puerto Rican.

But it was light all day, sweating hot — iron eyes blinking at the
    human element —

Irreducible Me today, I bought cigarettes at a machine, I was
    really worried

about my gross belly independent of philosophy, drama, idealism
    imagery —

My fate and I became one today and today became today —

just like a mystic prophecy — I'll conquer my belly tomorrow

or not, I'll toy with Mr. Choice also for real — today I said
    " Forever " thrice —

and walked under the vast Ladder of Doom, insouciant, not
    merely innocent

but completely hopeless! In Despair when I woke this morning,

my mouth furry smoked a Lucky Strike first thing when I dialed
    telephone to check on the Building Department —

I considered the License Department as I brushed my teeth with
    an odd toothbrush

some visitor left I lost mine — where? rack my brains it's there

somewhere in the past — with the snubnosed uncle cock from the
    freakshow

The old man familiar today, first time I thought of him in years,
    in the rain

in Massachusetts but I was a child that summer The pink thing bulged at his open thigh fly

he fingered it out to show me — I tarried till startled when the whiskied barker

questioned mine I ran out on the boardwalk drizzle confronting the Atlantic Ocean

— so trotted around the silent moody blocks home speechless

to mother father vaginal jelly rubber instruments discovered in the closet —

a stealthy memory makes hackles rise — " He inserts his penis into her vagina " —

What a weird explanation! I who collected matchbook covers like J. P. Morgan

gloating over sodden discoveries in the wet gutter — O happy grubby sewers of Revere — distasteful riches —

hopeless treasure I threw away in a week when I realized it was endless to complete —

next year gathered all the heat in my loins to spurt my white surprise drops into the wet brown wood under a

steamy shower, I used the toilet paper cardboard skeleton tube

to rub and thrill around my unconscious own shaft — playing with myself unbeknownst to the entire population of Far Rockaway —

remembered it all today — many years thinking of Kali-Ma and other matters —

a big surprise it was Me — Dear Reader, I seem strange to myself —

You recognise everything all over again where you are, it's wonderful

to be introduced to strangers who know you already —

like being Famous — a reverberation of Eternal Consciousness —

Today heraldic of Today, archetypal mimeograph machines reprinting everybody's poetry,

like finishing a book of surrealism which I haven't read for
    years —
Benjamin Peret & René Crevel heroic for real — the old New
    Consciousness reminded
me today — how busy I was, how fatal like a man in the
    madhouse, distracted
with presence of dishes of food to eat — Today's *" stringbeans
    in the moonlight "*
Like today I brought home blueberry pie for the first time in
    years —
Also today bit by a mosquito (to be precise, toward dawn)
(toward dusk ate marshmallows at the News Stand and drank
    huge cold grape soda eyeing :
this afternoon's *Journal* headline FBI IN HARLEM, what kind
    of Nasty old Epic
Afternoons I imagine !) Another event, a $10 bill in my hands,
    debt repaid,
a café expresso smaller event — Feeling rich I bought a second-
    hand record of Gertrude Stein's actual Voice —
My day was Harmonious — Though I heard no mechanic
    music —
I noticed some Nazi propaganda — I wrote down my dream
    about Earth dying — I wanted to telephone Long Island —
    I stood on a street corner and didn't know where to go —
I telephoned the Civil Liberties Union — discussed the Junk
    Problem & Supreme Court —
I thought I was planting suggestions in everybody's Me-ity —
thought a few minutes of Blake — his quatrains — I climbed
    four flights & stood at Fainlight's Chinatown door locked
    up — I'm being mysterious —
What does this mean? Don't ask me today, I'm still thinking,
Trying to remember what happened while it's still happening —

I wrote a " poem," I scribbled quotation marks everywhere
    over Fate passing by

Sometimes I felt noble, sometimes I felt ugly, I spoke to man and
    woman

from *Times* & *Time*, summarized hugely — plots, cinematic
    glories, I boasted a little, subtly —

Was I seen thru? Too much happened to see thru All —

I was never alone except for two blocks by the park, nor was I
    unhappy —

I blessed my Guru, I felt like a shyster — told Ed how much I
    liked being made love to by delicate girl hands —

It's true, more girls should do that to us, we chalked up another
    mark what's wrong

and told everybody to register to vote this November — I
    stopped on the street and shook hands —

I took a crap once this day — How extraordinary it all goes!
    recollected, a lifetime!

Imagine writing autobiography what a wealth of Detail to enlist!

I see the contents of future magazines — just a peek Today being
    hurried —

Today is slowly ending — I will step back into it and disappear.

July 21, 1964

MESSAGE II

Long since the years
letters songs Mantras
eyes apartments bellies
kissed and grey bridges
walked across in mist
Now your brother's Welfare's
paid by State now Lafcadio's
home with Mama, now you're
in NY beds with big poetic
girls & go picket on the street
I clang my finger-cymbals in Havana, I lie
with teenage boys afraid of the red police,
I jack off in Cuban modern bathrooms, I ascend
over blue oceans in a jet plane, the mist hides
the black synagogue, I will look for the Golem,
I hide under the clock near my hotel, it's intermission
for Tales of Hoffmann, nostalgia for the 19th century
rides through my heart like the music of Die Moldau,
I'm still alone with long black beard and shining eyes
walking down black smokey tramcar streets at night
past royal muscular statues on an old stone bridge,
Over the river again today in Breughel's wintery city,
the snow is white on all the rooftops of Prague,
Salute beloved comrade I'll send you my tears from Moscow.

March 1965

BIG BEAT

The *Olympics* have descended into
      red velvet basement
      theaters of Centrum
long long hair over skeleton boys
thin black ties, pale handsome
      cheeks — and screams and screams,
Orchestra mob ecstasy rising from
    this new generation of buttocks and eyes
             and tender nipples
Because the body moves again, the
      body dances again, the body
        sings again
    the body screams new-born after
War, infants cursed with secret cold
      jail deaths of the Fifties — Now
    girls with new breasts and striplings
    wearing soft golden puberty hair —
1000 voices scream five minutes long
clapping thousand handed in great ancient measure
saluting the Meat God of XX Century
that moves thru the theater like the
      secret rhythm of the belly in
          Orgasm
Kalki! Apocalypse Christ! Maitreya! grim
    Chronos weeps
        tired into the **saxophone,**
The Earth is Saved! Next number!
    SHE'S A WOMAN
        Electric guitar red bells!

and Ganymede emerges stomping
      his feet for Joy on the stage
  and bows to the ground, and weeping, GIVES.
Oh the power of the God on his throne
      constantly surrounded by white drums
  right hand Sceptered beating brass cymbals !

March 11, 1965

CAFE IN WARSAW

These spectres resting on plastic stools
leather-gloved spectres flitting thru the coffeehouse one hour
spectre girls with scarred faces, black stockings thin eyebrows
spectre boys blond hair combed neat over the skull little chin
    beards
new spectres talking intensely crowded together over black shiny
    tables late afternoon
the sad soprano of history chanting thru a hi-fidelity loudspeaker
— perspective walls & windows 18th century down New
    World Avenue to Sigmund III column'd
sword upraised watching over Polish youth 3 centuries —
O Polish spectres what've you suffered since Chopin wept into
    his romantic piano
old buildings rubbled down, gaiety of all night parties under the
    air bombs,
first screams of the vanishing ghetto — Workmen step thru
    prewar pink-blue bedroom walls demolishing sunny ruins —
Now spectres gather to kiss hands, girls kiss lip to lip, red witch-
    hair from Paris
& fine gold watches — to sit by the yellow wall with a large
    brown briefcase —
to smoke three cigarettes with thin black ties and nod heads over
    a new movie —
Spectres Christ and your bodies be with you for this hour while
    you're young
in postwar heaven stained with the sweat of Communism, your
    loves and your white smooth cheekskin soft in the glance of
    each other's eye.
O spectres how beautiful your calm shaven faces, your pale

lipstick scarves, your delicate heels,

how beautiful your absent gaze, legs crossed alone at table with long eyelashes,

how beautiful your patient love together sitting reading the art journals —

how beautiful your entrance thru the velvet-curtained door, laughing into the overcrowded room,

how you wait in your hats, measure the faces, and turn and depart for an hour,

or meditate at the bar, waiting for the slow waitress to prepare red hot tea, minute by minute

standing still as hours ring in churchbells, as years pass and you will remain in Novy Swiat,

how beautiful you press your lips together, sigh forth smoke from your mouth, rub your hands

or lean together laughing to notice this wild haired madman who sits weeping among you a stranger.

4/10/65

THE MOMENTS RETURN

a thousand sunsets behind tramcar wires in open skies of Warsaw

Palace of Culture chinese peaks blacken against the orange-clouded horizon —

an iron trolley rolling insect antennae sparks blue overhead, hat man limping past rusty apartment walls —

Christ under white satin gleam in chapels — trembling fingers on the long rosary — awaiting resurrection

Old red fat Jack mortal in Florida — tears in black eyelash, Bach's farewell to the Cross —

That was 24 years ago on a scratchy phonograph Sebastian Sampas bid adieu to earth —

I stopped on the pavement to remember the Warsaw Concerto, hollow sad pianos crashing like bombs, celestial tune

in a kitchen in Ozone Park — It all came true in the sunset on a deserted street —

And I have nothing to do this evening but walk in a fur coat on the cool grey avenue years later, a melancholy man alone —

the music fading to another universe — the moments return — **reverberations of taxicabs arriving at a park bench** —

My beard is misery, no language to these young eyes — that I remember myself naked in my earliest dream —

now sat by the car-crossing rueful of the bald front of my skull and the grey sign of time in my beard —

headache or dancing exhaustion or dysentery in Moscow or vomit in New York —

Oh — the Metropol Hotel is built — crowds waiting on traffic islands under streetlamp — the cry of tramcars on Jerusalemski —

Roof towers flash Red State — the vast stone avenue hung with
    yellow bulbs — stop lights blink, long trolleys grind to
    rest, motorcycles pass exploding —

The poem returns to the moment, my vow to record — my cold
    fingers — & must sit and wait for my own lone Presence —
    the first psalm —

I also return to myself, the moment and I are one man on a park
    bench on a crowded streetcorner in Warsaw —

I breathe and sigh — *Give up desire for children* the bony-faced
    white bearded Guru said in Benares — am I ready to die?

or a voice at my side on the bench, a gentle question — worn
    young man's face under pearl grey hat —

Alas, all I can say is " No Panamay " — I can't speak.

Easter Sunday 4/18/65

KRAL MAJALES

And the Communists have nothing to offer but fat cheeks and
    eyeglasses and lying policemen
and the Capitalists proffer Napalm and money in green suitcases
    to the Naked,
and the Communists create heavy industry but the heart is also
    heavy
and the beautiful engineers are all dead, the secret technicians
    conspire for their own glamor
in the Future, in the Future, but now drink vodka and lament
    the Security Forces,
and the Capitalists drink gin and whiskey on airplanes but let
    Indian brown millions starve
and when Communist and Capitalist assholes tangle the Just
    man is arrested or robbed or had his head cut off,
but not like Kabir, and the cigarette cough of the Just man
    above the clouds
in the bright sunshine is a salute to the health of the blue sky.
For I was arrested thrice in Prague, once for singing drunk on
    Narodni street,
once knocked down on the midnight pavement by a mustached
    agent who screamed out BOUZERANT,
once for losing my notebooks of unusual sex politics dream
    opinions,
and I was sent from Havana by plane by detectives in green
    uniform,
and I was sent from Prague by plane by detectives in
    Czechoslovakian business suits,
Cardplayers out of Cezanne, the two strange dolls that entered
    Joseph K's room at morn

also entered mine, and ate at my table, and examined my
  scribbles,

and followed me night and morn from the houses of lovers to
  the cafés of Centrum —

And I am the King of May, which is the power of sexual youth,

and I am the King of May, which is industry in eloquence and
  action in amour,

and I am the King of May, which is long hair of Adam and the
  Beard of my own body

and I am the King of May, which is Kral Majales in the Czecho-
  slovakian tongue,

and I am the King of May, which is old Human poesy, and
  100,000 people chose my name,

and I am the King of May, and in a few minutes I will land at
  London Airport,

and I am the King of May, naturally, for I am of Slavic
  parentage and a Buddhist Jew

who worships the Sacred Heart of Christ the blue body of
  Krishna the straight back of Ram

the beads of Chango the Nigerian singing Shiva Shiva in a
  manner which I have invented,

and the King of May is a middleeuropean honor, mine in the
  XX century

despite space ships and the Time Machine, because I heard the
  voice of Blake in a vision,

and repeat that voice. And I am King of May that sleeps with
  teenagers laughing.

And I am the King of May, that I may be expelled from my
  Kingdom with Honor, as of old,

To shew the difference between Caesar's Kingdom and the
  Kingdom of the May of Man —

and I am the King of May, tho paranoid, for the Kingdom of

    May is too beautiful to last for more than a month —

and I am the King of May because I touched my finger to my
    forehead saluting

a luminous heavy girl trembling hands who said " one moment
    Mr. Ginsberg "

before a fat young Plainclothesman stepped between our bodies
    — I was going to England —

and I am the King of May, returning to see Bunhill Fields and
    walk on Hampstead Heath,

and I am the King of May, in a giant jetplane touching Albion's
    airfield trembling in fear

as the plane roars to a landing on the grey concrete, shakes &
    expels air,

and rolls slowly to a stop under the clouds with part of blue
    heaven still visible.

And *tho* I am the King of May, the Marxists have beat me upon
    the street, kept me up all night in Police Station, followed
    me thru Springtime Prague, detained me in secret and
    deported me from our kingdom by airplane.

Thus I have written this poem on a jet seat in mid Heaven.

May 7, 1965

GURU

It is the moon that disappears
It is the stars that hide not I
It's the City that vanishes, I stay
with my forgotten shoes,
my invisible stocking
It is the call of a bell

Primrose Hill May '65

DROWSE MURMURS

. . . touch of vocal flattery
exists where you wake us
at dawn with happy sphinx
lids eyeball heavy anchored
together in mysterious Signature,
this is the end of the world
whether Atom bomb hits
it or I fall down death
alone no body help help
It's me myself caught in throes
of Ugh ! They got me whom you lately loved
of soft cloth beds to stick his cock
in the wrong way lost animal, what wd Zoology
say on Park Bench watching the Spectacle
of this time Me it's my body going to die,
it's My ship sinking forever, O Captain
the fearful trip is done ! I'm all alone,
This is human, and the cat that licks its ass
also hath short term to be furry specter
as I do woken by last thought leap
up from my pillow as the cat leaps up
on the desk chair to resolve its foot lick,
I lick my own mind observe the pipe
crawling up the brick wall, see picture
room-sides hung with nails emblem
abstract oil funny glyphs, girls
naked, letters & newspapers the World
Map coloured over for emphasis somebody born —
my thoughts almost lost, I absorb the big

earth lamps hung from the ceiling for ready light,
hear the chirp of birds younger than I
and faster doomed, that jet plane whistle
hiss roar above roofs stronger winged
than any thin-jawed bird — the precise robot
for air flying's stronger than me even,
tho metal fatigue may come before I'm 90 —
I scratch my hairy skull and lean on elbow bone
as alarm clock Sat Morn rings next door
and wakes a sleeper body to face his day.
How amazing here, now this time newspaper
history, when earth planet they say revolves
around one sun that on outer Galaxy arm
revolves center so vast slow pinwheel
big this speckless invisible molecule I am
sits up solid motionless early dawn thinking
high in every direction photograph spiral nebula
photograph death BLANK photograph this wakened
brick minute bird-song pipe-flush elbow lean
in soft pillow to scribe the green sign Paradis.

June 1965

WHO BE KIND TO

Be kind to your self, it is only one
    and perishable
of many on the planet, thou art that
one that wishes a soft finger tracing the
    line of feeling from nipple to pubes —
one that wishes a tongue to kiss your armpit,
    a lip to kiss your cheek inside your
    whiteness thigh —
Be kind to yourself Harry, because unkindness
    comes when the body explodes
napalm cancer and the deathbed in Vietnam
is a strange place to dream of   trees
    leaning over and angry American faces
grinning with sleepwalk terror over your
    last eye —
Be kind to yourself, because the bliss of your own
    kindness will flood the police tomorrow,
because the cow weeps in the field and the
    mouse weeps in the cat hole —
Be kind to this place, which is your present
    habitation, with derrick and radar tower
    and flower in the ancient brook —
Be kind to your neighbor who weeps
    solid tears on the television sofa,
he has no other home, and hears nothing
    but the hard voice of telephones
Click, buzz, switch channel and the inspired
    melodrama disappears
and he's left alone for the night, he disappears
    in bed —

Be kind to your disappearing mother and
     father gazing out the terrace window
     as milk truck and hearse turn the corner
Be kind to the politician weeping in the galleries
     of Whitehall, Kremlin, White House
     Louvre and Phoenix City
aged, large nosed, angry, nervously dialing
     the bald voice connected to
electrodes underground converging thru
     wires vaster than a kitten's eye can see
on the mushroom shaped fear-lobe under
     the ear of Sleeping Dr. Einstein
crawling with worms, crawling with worms, crawling
     with worms the hour has come —
Sick, dissatisfied, unloved, the bulky
     foreheads of Captain Premier President
     Sir Comrade Fear!
Be kind to the fearful one at your side
     Who's remembering the Lamentations
     of the bible
the prophesies of the Crucified Adam   Son
     of all the porters and char men of
             Bell   gravia —
Be kind to your self who weeps under
     the Moscow moon and hide your bliss hairs
     under raincoat and suede Levis —
For this is the joy to be born, the kindness
     received thru strange eyeglasses on
     a bus thru Kensington,
the finger touch of the Londoner on your thumb,
     that borrows light from your cigarette,
the morning smile at Newcastle Central

station, when longhair Tom blond husband
    greets the bearded stranger of telephones —
the boom bom that bounces in the joyful
    bowels as the Liverpool Minstrels of
    CavernSink
raise up their joyful voices and guitars
    in electric Afric hurrah
    for Jerusalem —
The saints come marching in, Twist &
    Shout, and Gates of Eden are named
    in Albion again
Hope sings a black psalm from Nigeria,
    and a white psalm echoes in Detroit
    and reechoes amplified from Nottingham to Prague
and a Chinese psalm will be heard, if we all
    live out our lives for the next 6 decades —
Be kind to the Chinese psalm in the red transistor
    in your breast —
Be kind to the Monk in the 5 Spot who plays
    lone chord-bangs on his vast piano
lost in space on a bench and hearing himself
    in the nightclub universe —
Be kind to the heroes that have lost their
    names in the newspaper
and hear only their own supplication for
    the peaceful kiss of sex in the giant
    auditoriums of the planet,
nameless voices crying for kindness in the orchestra,
screaming in anguish that bliss come true
    and sparrows sing another hundred years
    to white haired babes
and poets be fools of their own desire — O Anacreon

and angelic Shelley !
Guide these new-nippled generations on space
    ships to Mars' next universe
The prayer is to man and girl, the only
    gods, the only lords of Kingdoms of
    Feeling, Christs of their own
    living ribs —
Bicycle chain and machine gun, fear sneer
    & smell cold logic of the Dream Bomb
have come to Saigon, **Johannesburg,**
    Dominica City, Pnom-Penh, Pentagon
    Paris and Lhasa —
Be kind to the universe of Self that
    trembles and shudders and thrills
    in XX Century,
that opens its eyes and belly and breast
    chained with flesh to feel
    the myriad flowers of bliss
    that I Am to Thee —
A dream ! a Dream ! I don't want to be alone !
    I want to know that I am loved !
I want the orgy of our flesh, orgy
    of all eyes happy, orgy of the soul
    kissing and blessing its mortal-grown
    body,
orgy of tenderness beneath the neck, orgy of
    kindness to thigh and vagina
Desire given with meat hand
    and cock, desire taken with
    mouth and ass, desire returned
    to the last sigh !
Tonite let's all make love in London

as if it were 2001 the years
of thrilling god —
And be kind to the poor soul that cries in
a crack of the pavement because he
has no body —
Prayers to the ghosts and demons, the
lackloves of Capitals & Congresses
who make sadistic noises
on the radio —
Statue destroyers & tank captains, unhappy
murderers in Mekong & Stanleyville,
That a new kind of man has come to his bliss
to end the cold war he has borne
against his own kind flesh
since the days of the snake.

June 8, 1965

STUDYING THE SIGNS
After Reading Briggflatts

White light's wet glaze on asphalt city floor,
the *Guinness Time* house clock hangs sky misty,
yellow *Cathay* food lamps blink, rain falls
on rose neon *Swiss Watch* under Regent archway,
Sun Alliance and London Insurance Group stands
granite — " Everybody gets torn down " ... as a high
black taxi with orange doorlight passes around
iron railing blazoned with red sigma *Underground* —
Ah where the cars glide slowly round Eros
shooting down on one who stands in Empire's Hub
under his shining silver breast, look at Man's
sleepy face under half-spread metal wings —
Swan & Edgar's battlement walls the moving Circus,
princely high windows barred (shadow bank
interior office stairway marble) behind castiron
green balconies emblemed with single swans afloat
like white teacups what — *Boots'* blue sign lit up
over an enamel weight-machine's mirror clockface
at door betwixt plateglass *Revlon* & slimming bisquit
plaques and that alchemical blood-crimson pharmacy
bottle perched on street display. *A Severed Head*
" relished uproariously " above the masq'd *Criterion*
marquee, with Thespis and Ceres plaster Graces lifting
white arms in the shelled niches above a fire gong
on the wooden-pillared facade whose mansard gables
lean in blue-black sky drizzle, thin flagpole.
Like the prow of a Queen Mary the curved building
sign *Players* package, blue capped center

Navvy encircled by his life-belt a sweet bearded
profile against 19'th century sea waves —
last a giant red delicious *Coca Cola* signature
covers half the building back to gold *Cathay.*
Cars stop three abreast for the light, race forward,
turtleneck youths jump the fence toward *Boots,*
the night-gang in Mod slacks and ties sip
coffee at the *Snac-A-Matic* corner opendoor,
a boy leaned under *Cartoon Cinema* lifts hand
puffs white smoke and waits agaze — a wakened
pigeon flutters down from streetlamp to the fountain,
primly walks and pecks the empty pave — now deep
blue planet-light dawns in Piccadilly's low sky.

June 12, 1965

PORTLAND COLISEUM

A brown   piano in diamond
    white spotlight
Leviathan auditorium
     iron rib wired
     hanging organs, vox
       black battery
A single whistling sound of
     ten thousand children's
       larynxes asinging
       pierce the ears
     and flowing up the belly
     bliss the moment arrived

Apparition, four brown English
     jacket christhair boys
Goofed Ringo battling bright
        white drums
Silent George hair patient
       Soul horse
Short black-skulled Paul
      wit thin guitar
Lennon the Captain, his mouth
     a triangular smile,
all jump together to End
     some tearful memory song
       ancient two years,

     The million children
     the thousand worlds
bounce in their seats, bash

       each other's sides, press
       legs together nervous
Scream again & claphand
       become one Animal
       in the New World Auditorium
    — hands waving myriad
        snakes of thought
       screetch beyond hearing

while a line of police with
       folded arms stands
Sentry to contain the red
       sweatered ecstasy
    that rises upward to the
         wired roof.

August 27, 1965

FIRST PARTY AT KEN KESEY'S WITH HELL'S ANGELS

Cool black night thru the redwoods
cars parked outside in shade
behind the gate, stars dim above
the ravine, a fire burning by the side
porch and a few tired souls hunched over
in black leather jackets. In the huge
wooden house, a yellow chandelier
at 3AM the blast of loudspeakers
hi-fi Rolling Stones Ray Charles Beatles
Jumping Joe Jackson and twenty youths
dancing to the vibration thru the floor,
a little weed in the bathroom, girls in scarlet
tights, one muscular smooth skinned man
sweating dancing for hours, beer cans
bent littering the yard, a hanged man
sculpture dangling from a high creek branch,
children sleeping softly in their bedroom bunks.
And 4 police cars parked outside the painted
gate, red lights revolving in the leaves.

December 1965

CARMEL VALLEY

Grass yellow hill,
        small mountain range blue sky
     bright reservoir below road tiny cars
The wing tree green wind sigh
        rises, falls —
    Buddha, Christ, fissiparous
            Tendencies —
White sun rays   pierce my eyeglasses —
    grey bark animal arms,
           skin peeling,
     sprig fingers pointing, twigs trembling
       green plate-thins bobbing,
          knotted branch-sprouts —
No one will have to announce New Age
No special name, no Unique way,
    no crier by Method or
         Herald of Snakey Unknown,
No Messiah necessary but the Country ourselves
        fifty years old —
Allah this tree, Eternity this Space Age!
Teenagers walking on Times Sq. look up
    at blue planets thru neon metal
            buildingtops,
Old men lay on grass afternoons
    old Walnut stands on green mountain hide,
        ants crawl the page, invisible
       insects sing, birds
           flap down,
Man will relax on a hill remembering tree friends.
11/65 — Chez Baez

A VISION IN HOLLYWOOD

Here at the atomic Crack-end of Time XX Century
History swifting past horse chariot earth wheel
So I in mid-age, finished with half desire
Tranquil in my hairy body, familiar beard face,
                              Same fingers to pen
                              as twenty years ago began
                        scribbled Confession to fellow Beings
                        Americans —
                                    Heavenly creatures,

This universe a thing of dream
              substance naught & Keystone void
                        vibrations of symmetry Yes   No
                        Foundation of Gold Element Atom
              all the way down to the first Wave
              making opposite Nothing a mirror
which begat a wave of Ladies marrying
waves of Gentlemen till I was born in 1926
              in Newark, New Jersey under the sign
                                    sweet Gemini —

Whole universes hived upon the first
              dumb Jerk
                        that wasn't there — The
Only One escape from the black Not Ever
was Itself,
              a extra click of Life woke
because Nothing had no hand to switch off
the Light.

The first dumb Jerk,
one wave, Forward! one way too many —
So forward got backward, & Sideways both
            got there simultaneous with up
                        and down who got each other
Meanwhile the first Being got its non-Being
            Opposite which never had to be there before
This calamity, this accident, this Goof,
            this Imperceptible Sneak of Dimension,
                        Some Move-Push tickle, Aleph or Aum
                                    swallowed before uttered,
                        one-eyed sparkle, giant glint, any tiny fart
                        or rose-whiff before roses were
                                    Thought Impossible
filled every corner of Emptiness with Symmetries of
            Impossible Universe with no Idea
How Come, & Opposite Possible Kosmoses
                        assembled Doubtless —
One makes two, symmetry's infinite touch
makes Sound bounce, light sees
                        waves reproduce oceans,
            vibrations are red white & blue —

            All like a 3 dimensional TV dream
            like Science-fiction opera
                        sung by inexistent Gas-brains
                                    in their N-dimensional bag,
            Some what a bubble, some what dewdrop
            Some what a blossom, some what
                                    lightning flash,
            Some what the old Jew in the Hospital —
                        snap of dying fingers,

" Where did it all *go* ? "

Made of Ideas, waves, dots, hot projectors
mirror movie screens,
      Some what the Shadow cast at Radio City
                     Music Hall Xmas 1939
gone, gone, utterly completely gone
to a world of Snow
      White and the Seven Dwarfs —
Made up of cartoon picture clouds, paper maché
        Japanese lantern stage sets strung
    with moon lights, neon arc-flames,
      electric switches, thunder
reverberating from phonograph record tape machine
      Tin sheets of Zeus on
the Microphone jacked to gigantic Amplifiers, gauge
    needle jumping, red lights warning Other
Dimensions off the overloaded public address Sound
    Systems feedback thru blue void
      echoing the Real of Endless Film.

Xmas 1965

CHANCES " R "

Nymph and shepherd raise electric tridents
       glowing red against the plaster wall,
The jukebox beating out magic syllables,
A line of painted boys snapping fingers
         & shaking thin Italian trouserlegs
             or rough dungarees on big asses
                bumping and dipping
ritually, with no religion but the
          old one of cocksuckers
naturally, in Kansas center of America
       the farmboys in Diabolic bar light
     alone stiff necked or lined up
     dancing row on row like Afric husbands
& the music's sad here, whereas Sunset Trip or
Jukebox Corner it's ecstatic pinball machines —
Religiously, with concentration and free
          prayer; fairy boys of the plains
          and their gay sisters of the city
step together to the center of the floor
       illumined by machine eyes, screaming drumbeats,
         passionate voices of Oklahoma City
           chanting No Satisfaction
Suspended from Heaven the Chances R
     Club floats rayed by stars
       along a Wichita tree avenue
     traversed with streetlights on the plain.

February 1966

WICHITA VORTEX SUTRA
I

Turn Right Next Corner
>> *The Biggest Little Town in Kansas*
>>> *Macpherson*
Red sun setting flat plains west streaked
>> with gauzy veils, chimney mist spread
>> around christmas-tree bulbed refineries — aluminum
>> white tanks squat beneath
>> winking signal towers' bright plane-lights,
>>> orange gas flares
>> beneath pillows of smoke, flames in machinery —
>>> transparent towers at dusk

In advance of the Cold Wave
>> *Snow is spreading eastward to*
>>> *the Great Lakes*
> News Broadcast & old clarinets
>> Watertower dome Lighted on the flat plain
>>> car radio speeding acrost railroad tracks —

Kansas! Kansas! Shuddering at last!
>> PERSON appearing in Kansas!
> angry telephone calls to the University
Police dumbfounded leaning on
>> their radiocar hoods
> While Poets chant to Allah in the roadhouse Showboat!
Blue eyed children dance and hold thy Hand O aged Walt
>> who came from Lawrence to Topeka to envision
>>> Iron interlaced upon the city plain —

Telegraph wires strung from city to city O Melville!
           Television brightening thy *rills of Kansas lone*
I come,
        lone man from the void, riding a bus
        hypnotized by red tail lights on the straight
                    space road ahead —
  & the Methodist minister with cracked eyes
                leaning over the table
          quoting Kierkegaard ' death of God '
                  a million dollars
    in the bank   owns all West Wichita
                  come to Nothing!
        Prajnaparamita Sutra over coffee — Vortex
of telephone radio aircraft assembly frame ammunition
petroleum nightclub Newspaper streets illuminated by Bright
                EMPTINESS —

Thy sins are forgiven, Wichita!
        Thy lonesomeness annulled, O Kansas dear!
          as the western Twang prophesied
    thru banjo, when lone cowboy walked the railroad track
          past an empty station toward the sun
      sinking giant-bulbed orange down the box canyon —
  Music strung over his back
      and empty handed   singing on this planet earth
            I'm a lonely Dog, O Mother!
Come, Nebraska, sing & dance with me —
    Come lovers of Lincoln and Omaha,
          hear my soft voice at last
As Babes need the chemical touch of flesh in pink infancy
    lest they die Idiot returning to Inhuman —
                Nothing —

So, tender lipt adolescent girl, pale youth,

> give me back my soft kiss

> Hold me in your innocent arms,

>> accept my tears as yours to harvest

>> equal   in nature to the Wheat

> that made your bodies' muscular bones

>> broad shouldered, boy bicept —

> from leaning on cows & drinking Milk

>> in Midwest Solitude —

No more fear of tenderness, much delight in weeping, ecstasy

> in singing, laughter rises that confounds

>> staring Idiot mayors

>>> and stony politicians eyeing

>> Thy breast,

>>> O Man of America, be born!

Truth breaks through!

> How big is the prick of the President?

> How big is Cardinal Viet-Nam?

How little the prince of the F.B.I., unmarried all these years!

> How big are all the Public Figures?

What kind of flesh hangs, hidden behind their Images?

>>> Approaching Salina,

Prehistoric excavation, *Apache Uprising*

>> in the drive-in theater

> Shelling Bombing Range   mapped in the distance,

> Crime Prevention Show, sponsor Wrigley's Spearmint

> Dinosaur Sinclair advertisement, glowing green —

South 9th Street lined with poplar & elm branch

>> spread over evening's tiny headlights —

> **Salina Highschool's brick darkens Gothic**

>> over a night-lit door —

What wreaths of naked bodies, thighs and faces,
                 small hairy bun'd vaginas,
                 silver cocks, armpits and breasts
           moistened by tears
                      for 20 years, for 40 years?
Peking Radio surveyed by Luden's Coughdrops
                 Attacks on the Russians & Japanese,
Big Dipper leaning above the Nebraska border,
                 handle down to the blackened plains,
       telephone-pole ghosts crossed
                           by roadside, dim headlights —
       dark night, & giant T-bone steaks,
             and in *The Village Voice*
           New Frontier Productions present
                   Camp Comedy : *Fairies I Have Met.*
Blue highway lamps strung along the horizon east at Hebron
             Homestead National Monument near Beatrice —

Language, language
           black Earth-circle in the rear window,
                     no cars for miles along highway
             beacon lights on oceanic plain
       language, language
                   over Big Blue River
               chanting *La Illaha El ('lill) Allah Who*
             revolving my head to my heart like my mother
               chin abreast at Allah
                   Eyes closed, blackness
vaster than midnight prairies,
             Nebraskas of solitary Allah,
                 Joy, I am I

the lone One singing to myself
                                        God come true—
                        Thrills of fear,
                nearer than the vein in my neck — ?
What if I opened my soul to sing to my absolute self
        Singing as the car crash chomped thru blood & muscle
                                                tendon skull?
        What if I sang, and loosed the chords of fear brow?
                What exquisite noise wd

                                shiver my car companions?
                I am the Universe tonite
                        riding in all my Power riding
chauffeured thru my self by a long haired saint with eyeglasses
What if I sang till Students knew I was free
        of Viet-Nam, trousers, free of my own meat,
        free to die in my thoughtful shivering Throne?
                freer than Nebraska, freer than America,
                        May I disappear
                in magic Joy-smoke! Pouf! reddish Vapor,
Faustus vanishes weeping & laughing
        under stars on Highway 77 between Beatrice & Lincoln —
        " Better not to move but let things be " Reverend Preacher?
                        We've all already disappeared!

Space highway open, entering Lincoln's ear
        ground to a stop Tracks Warning
                        Pioneer Boulevard —
        William Jennings Bryan sang
        Thou shalt not crucify mankind upon a cross of Gold!
                        O Baby Doe! Gold's
        Department Store hulks o'er 10th Street now
        — an unregenerate old fop who didn't want to be a monkey

now's the Highest Perfect Wisdom dust
        and Lindsay's cry
    survives compassionate in the Highschool Anthology —
a giant dormitory brilliant on the evening plain
                drifts with his memories —
There's a nice white door over there
            for me O dear!   on Zero Street.
February 15, 1966

II

Face the Nation
Thru Hickman's rolling earth hills
        icy winter
            grey sky   bare trees lining the road
    South to Wichita
       you're in the Pepsi Generation   Signum enroute
Aiken Republican on the radio   60,000
      Northvietnamese troops now infiltrated but over 250,000
      South Vietnamese   armed men
              our Enemy —
                Not Hanoi our enemy
                Not China our enemy
                  The Viet Cong!
           MacNamara made a " bad guess "
" Bad Guess " chorused the Reporters?
    Yes, no more than a Bad Guess, in 1962
              " 8000 American Troops handle the
                  Situation "

Bad Guess

in 1956, 80% of the
Vietnamese people would've voted for Ho Chi Minh
wrote Ike   years later   *Mandate for Change*
A bad guess in the Pentagon
And the Hawks were guessing all along
Bomb China's 200,000,000
cried Stennis from Mississippi
I guess it was 3 weeks ago
Holmes Alexander in Albuquerque Journal
Provincial newsman
said I guess we better begin to do that Now.
his typewriter clacking in his aged office
on a side street   under Sandia Mountain?
Half the world away from China
Johnson got some bad advice   Republican Aiken sang
to the Newsmen over the radio
The General guessed they'd stop infiltrating the South
if they bombed the North —
So I guess they bombed!
Pale Indochinese boys came thronging thru the jungle
in increased numbers
to the scene of TERROR!
While the triangle-roofed Farmer's Grain Elevator
sat quietly by the side of the road
along the railroad track
American Eagle beating its wings over Asia
million dollar helicopters
a billion dollars worth of Marines
who loved *Aunt Betty*
Drawn from the shores and farms shaking
from the high schools to the landing barge

     blowing the air thru their cheeks with fear
        in *Life* on Television
Put it this way on the radio
Put it this way in television language
        Use the words
          language, language :
            " A bad guess "

Put it this way in headlines
    Omaha World Herald — *Rusk Says Toughness*
            Essential For Peace
Put it this way
    Lincoln Nebraska morning Star —
          Vietnam War Brings Prosperity
Put it *this* way
      Declared MacNamara,   speaking language
      Asserted Maxwell Taylor
      General, Consultant to White House
    Vietcong losses leveling up three five zero zero
             per month
    Front page testimony February '66
   Here in Nebraska same as Kansas same known in Saigon
      in Peking, in Moscow, same known
    by the youths of Liverpool three five zero zero
    the latest quotation in the human meat market —
        Father I cannot tell a lie !

A black horse bends its head to the stubble
    beside the silver stream winding thru the woods
    by an antique red barn on the outskirts of Beatrice —
        Quietness, quietness
     over this countryside
       except for unmistakable signals on radio

followed by the honkytonk tinkle
of a city piano
to calm the nerves of taxpaying housewives of a Sunday morn.
Has anyone looked in the eyes of the dead?
U.S. Army recruiting service sign *Careers With A Future*
Is anyone living to look for future forgiveness?
Water hoses frozen on the street, the
Crowd gathered to see a strange happening garage —
Red flames on Sunday morning
in a quiet town!
Has anyone looked in the eyes of the wounded?
Have we seen but paper faces, Life Magazine?
Are screaming faces made of dots,
electric dots on Television —
fuzzy decibels registering
the mammal voiced howl
from the outskirts of Saigon to console model picture tubes
in Beatrice, in Hutchinson, in El Dorado
in historic Abilene
O inconsolable!

Stop, and eat more flesh.
" We will negotiate anywhere anytime "
said the giant President
Kansas City Times 2/14/66 : " Word reached U.S. authori-
ties that Thailand's leaders feared that in Honolulu Johnson
might have tried to persuade South Vietnam's rulers to ease
their stand against negotiating with the Viet Cong.

American officials said these fears were groundless and
Humphrey was telling the Thais so."
A.P. dispatch
The last week's paper is Amnesia.

Three five zero zero is numerals
Headline language poetry, nine decades after Democratic Vistas
      and the Prophecy of the Good Grey Poet
           Our nation " of the fabled damned "
               or else . . .
    Language, language
Ezra Pound the Chinese Written Character for truth
      defined as man standing by his word
         Word picture :   forked creature
                     Man
      standing by a box, birds flying out
         representing mouth speech
Ham Steak please waitress, in the warm cafe.
     Different from a bad guess.
             The war is language,
               language abused
                  for Advertisement,
              language used
         like magic for power on the planet:
Black Magic language,
      formulas for reality —
         Communism is a 9 letter word
            used by inferior magicians with
the wrong alchemical formula for transforming earth into gold
       — funky warlocks operating on guesswork,
            handmedown mandrake terminology
                 that never worked in 1956
       for grey-domed Dulles,
             brooding over at State,
      that never worked for Ike who knelt to take
        the magic wafer in his mouth
               from Dulles' hand

inside the church in Washington :
Communion of bum magicians
                    congress of failures from Kansas & Missouri
            working with the wrong equations
            Sorcerer's Apprentices who lost control
                    of the simplest broomstick in the world :
                            Language
O longhaired magician come home take care of your dumb helper
        before the radiation deluge floods your livingroom,
                        your magic errandboy's
                            just made a bad guess again
                that's lasted a whole decade.

N B C B S U P A P I N S L I F E
        Time Mutual presents
                World's Largest Camp Comedy :
                        Magic In Vietnam —
        reality turned inside out
                changing its sex in the Mass Media
                for 30 days, TV den and bedroom farce
Flashing pictures Senate Foreign Relations Committee room
        Generals faces flashing on and off screen
                                mouthing language
            State Secretary speaking nothing but language
        MacNamara declining to speak public language
            The President talking language,
                    Senators reinterpreting language
            General Taylor *Limited Objectives*
                        Owls from Pennsylvania
                Clark's Face *Open Ended*
                        Dove's *Apocalypse*
                        Morse's hairy ears

Stennis orating in Mississippi
            half billion chinamen crowding into the
                        polling booth,
        Clean shaven Gen. Gavin's image
                        imagining *Enclaves*
                Tactical Bombing the magic formula for
            a silver haired Symington :
Ancient Chinese apothegm :
                Old in vain.
        Hawks swooping thru the newspapers
                talons visible
        wings outspread in the giant updraft of hot air
                    loosing their dry screech in the skies
                        over the Capitol
Napalm and black clouds emerging in newsprint
        Flesh soft as a Kansas girl's
                    ripped open by metal explosion —
    three five zero zero   on the other side of the planet
                caught in barbed wire, fire ball
                bullet shock, bayonet electricity
    bomb blast terrific in skull & belly, shrapnelled
                        throbbing meat
While this American nation argues war :
                conflicting language, language
                        proliferating in airwaves
        filling the farmhouse ear, filling
                the City Manager's head in his oaken office
                the professor's head in his bed at midnight
                the pupil's head at the movies
                    blond haired, his heart throbbing with desire
                    for the girlish image bodied on the screen :
                        or smoking cigarettes

and watching Captain Kangaroo
that fabled damned of nations
prophecy come true —
Though the highway's straight,
dipping downward through low hills,
rising narrow on the far horizon
black cows browse in caked fields
ponds in the hollows lie frozen,
quietness.
Is this the land that started war on China?
This be the soil that thought Cold War for decades?
Are these nervous naked trees & farmhouses
the vortex
of oriental anxiety molecules
that've imagined   American Foreign Policy
and magick'd up paranoia in Peking
and curtains of living blood
surrounding far Saigon?
Are these the towns where the language emerged
from the mouths here
that makes a Hell of riots in Dominica
sustains the aging tyranny of Chiang in silent Taipeh city
Paid for the lost French war in Algeria
overthrew the Guatemalan polis in '54
maintaining United Fruit's banana greed
another thirteen years
for the secret prestige of the Dulles family lawfirm?

Here's Marysville —
a black railroad engine in the children's park,
at rest —

and the Track Crossing
    with Cotton Belt flatcars
        carrying autos west from Dallas
    Delaware & Hudson gondolas filled with power stuff —
    a line of boxcars far east as the eye can see
        carrying battle goods to cross the Rockies
      into the hands of rich longshoremen loading
           ships on the Pacific —
    Oakland Army Terminal lights
        blue illumined all night now —
Crash of couplings and the great American train
    moves on carrying its cushioned load of metal doom
  Union Pacific linked together with your Hoosier Line
    followed by passive Wabash
      rolling behind
    all Erie carrying cargo in the rear,
    Central Georgia's rust colored truck proclaiming
      The Right Way, concluding
the awesome poem writ by the train
    across northern Kansas,
    land which gave right of way
    to the massing of metal meant for explosion
      in Indochina —
Passing thru Waterville,
    Electronic machinery in the bus humming prophecy —
    paper signs blowing in cold wind,
      mid-Sunday afternoon's silence
        in town
    under frost-grey sky
      that covers the horizon —
That the rest of earth is unseen,
    an outer universe invisible,

Unknown except thru
                    language
                            airprint
                                    magic images
or prophecy of the secret
                    heart the same
                    in Waterville as Saigon one human form :
            When a woman's heart bursts in Waterville
                            a woman screams equal in Hanoi —
On to Wichita to prophesy! O frightful Bard !
            into the heart of the Vortex
                    where anxiety rings
                            the University with millionaire pressure,
                    lonely crank telephone voices sighing in dread,
            and students waken trembling in their beds
                    with dreams of a new truth warm as meat,
                    little girls suspecting their elders of murder
                            committed by remote control machinery,
                    boys with sexual bellies aroused
                            chilled in the heart by the mailman
                    with a letter from an aging white haired General
                            Director of selection for service in
                                            Deathwar
                    all this black language
                            writ by machine !
                            O hopeless Fathers and Teachers
                            in Hué   do you know
                                    the same woe too?

I'm an old man now, and a lonesome man in Kansas
            but not afraid
                    to speak my lonesomeness in a car,

because not only my lonesomeness
it's Ours, all over America,
O tender fellows —
& spoken lonesomeness is Prophecy
in the moon 100 years ago or in
the middle of Kansas now.
It's not the vast plains mute our mouths
that fill at midnite with ecstatic language
when our trembling bodies hold each other
breast to breast on a mattress —
Not the empty sky that hides
the feeling from our faces
nor our skirts and trousers that conceal
the bodylove emanating in a glow of beloved skin,
white smooth abdomen down to the hair
between our legs,
It's not a God that bore us that forbid
our Being, like a sunny rose
all red with naked joy
between our eyes & bellies, yes
All we do is for this frightened thing
we call Love, want and lack —
fear that we aren't the one whose body could be
beloved of all the brides of Kansas City,
kissed all over by every boy of Wichita —
O but how many in their solitude weep aloud like me —
On the bridge over Republican River
almost in tears to know
how to speak the right language —
on the frosty broad road
uphill between highway embankments
I search for the language

that is also yours —
almost all our language has been taxed by war.
Radio antennae high tension
wires ranging from Junction City across the plains —
highway cloverleaf sunk in a vast meadow
lanes curving past Abilene
to Denver filled with old
heroes of love —
to Wichita where McClure's mind
burst into animal beauty
drunk, getting laid in a car
in a neon misted street
15 years ago —
to Independence where the old man's still alive
who loosed the bomb that's slaved all human consciousness
and made the body universe a place of fear —
Now, speeding along the empty plain,
no giant demon machine
visible on the horizon
but tiny human trees and wooden houses at the sky's edge
I claim my birthright!
reborn forever as long as Man
in Kansas or other universe — Joy
reborn after the vast sadness of War Gods!
A lone man talking to myself, no house in the brown vastness to hear,
imagining the throng of Selves
that make this nation one body of Prophecy
languaged by Declaration as
Happiness!
I call all Powers of imagination
to my side in this auto to make Prophecy,
all Lords

of human kingdoms to come
Shambu Bharti Baba naked covered with ash
Khaki Baba fat-bellied mad with the dogs
Dehorahava Baba who moans Oh how wounded, How wounded
Citaram Onkar Das Thakur who commands
give up your desire
Satyananda who raises two thumbs in tranquillity
Kali Pada Guha Roy whose yoga drops before the void
Shivananda who touches the breast and says OM
Srimata Krishnaji of Brindaban who says take for your guru
William Blake the invisible father of English visions
Sri Ramakrishna master of ecstasy eyes
half closed who only cries for his mother
Chaitanya arms upraised singing & dancing his own praise
merciful Chango judging our bodies
Durga-Ma covered with blood
destroyer of battlefield illusions
million-faced Tathagata gone past suffering
Preserver Harekrishna returning in the age of pain
Sacred Heart my Christ acceptable
Allah the Compassionate One
Jaweh Righteous One
all Knowledge-Princes of Earth-man, all
ancient Seraphim of heavenly Desire, Devas, yogis
& holymen I chant to —
Come to my lone presence
into this Vortex named Kansas,
I lift my voice aloud,
make Mantra of American language now,
I here declare the end of the War!
Ancient days' Illusion! —
and pronounce words beginning my own millennium.

Let the States tremble,
     let the Nation weep,
          let Congress legislate its own delight
               let the President execute his own desire —
this Act done by my own voice,
                   nameless Mystery —
published to my own senses,
               blissfully received by my own form
       approved with pleasure by my sensations
          manifestation of my very thought
          accomplished in my own imagination
               all realms within my consciousness fulfilled
       60 miles from Wichita
                 near El Dorado,
                     The Golden One,
in chill earthly mist
       houseless brown farmland plains rolling heavenward
                       in every direction
one midwinter afternoon Sunday called the day of the Lord —
       Pure Spring Water gathered in one tower
               where Florence is
                     set on a hill,
             stop for tea & gas

       Cars passing their messages along country crossroads
          to populaces cement-networked on flatness,
                 giant white mist on earth
         and a Wichita Eagle-Beacon headlines
           " Kennedy Urges Cong Get Chair in Negotiations "
The War is gone,
       Language emerging on the motel news stand,
                    the right magic

Formula, the language known
in the back of the mind before, now in black print
daily consciousness
Eagle News Services Saigon —
Headline Surrounded Vietcong Charge Into Fire Fight
the suffering not yet ended
for others
The last spasms of the dragon of pain
shoot thru the muscles
a crackling around the eyeballs
of a sensitive yellow boy by a muddy wall
Continued from page one   area
after the Marines killed 256 Vietcong captured 31
ten day operation Harvest Moon last December
Language language
U.S. Military Spokesmen
Language language
Cong death toll
has soared to 100 in First Air Cavalry
Division's Sector of
Language language
Operation White Wing near Bong Son
Some of the
Language language
Communist
Language language soldiers
charged so desperately
they were struck with six or seven bullets before they fell
Language Language M 60 Machine Guns
Language language in La Drang Valley
the terrain is rougher infested with leeches and scorpions
The war was over several hours ago !

Oh at last again the radio opens
      blue Invitations!
            Angelic Dylan singing across the nation
                  " When all your children start to resent you
                     Won't you come see me, Queen Jane? "
      His youthful voice making glad
                  the brown endless meadows
      His tenderness penetrating aether,
          soft prayer on the airwaves,
               Language language, and sweet music too
               even unto thee,
                  hairy flatness!
               even unto thee
                     despairing Burns!

Future speeding on swift wheels
            straight to the heart of Wichita!
Now radio voices cry population hunger world
                 of unhappy people
      waiting for Man to be born
             O man in America!
      you certainly smell good
               the radio says
passing mysterious families of winking towers
grouped round a quonset-hut on a hillock —
         feed storage or military fear factory here?
Sensitive City, Ooh! Hamburger & Skelley's Gas
               lights feed man and machine,
    Kansas Electric Substation aluminum robot
         signals thru thin antennae towers
         above the empty football field
                     at Sunday dusk

to a solitary derrick that pumps oil from the unconscious
                            working night & day
          & factory gas-flares edge a huge golf course
                   where tired businessmen can come and play —
Cloverleaf, Merging Traffic East Wichita turnoff
                    McConnel Airforce Base
                              nourishing the city —
        Lights rising in the suburbs
        Supermarket Texaco brilliance starred
                  over streetlamp vertebrae on Kellogg,
            green jewelled traffic lights
                confronting the windshield,
Centertown ganglion entered !
            Crowds of autos moving with their lightshine,
            signbulbs winking in the driver's eyeball —
The human nest collected, neon lit,
               and sunburst signed
           for business as usual, except on the Lord's Day —
Redeemer Lutheran's three crosses lit on the lawn
                reminder of our sins
and Titsworth offers insurance on Hydraulic
by De Voors Guard's Mortuary for outmoded bodies
                of the human vehicle
          which no Titsworth of insurance will customise
                        for resale —
So home, traveller, past the newspaper language factory
        under Union Station railroad bridge on Douglas
        to the center of the Vortex, calmly returned
            to Hotel Eaton —
Carry Nation began the war on Vietnam here
               with an angry smashing axe
                  attacking Wine —

Here fifty years ago, by her violence
began a vortex of hatred that defoliated the Mekong Delta —
Proud Wichita ! vain Wichita
cast the first stone ! —
That murdered my mother
who died of the communist anticommunist psychosis
in the madhouse one decade long ago
complaining about wires of masscommunication in her head
and phantom political voices in the air
besmirching her girlish character.
Many another has suffered death and madness
in the Vortex from Hydraulic
to the end of 17th — enough !
The war is over now —
Except for the souls
held prisoner in Niggertown
still pining for love of your tender white bodies O children of
Wichita !

UPTOWN

Yellow-lit Budweiser signs over oaken bars,
" I've seen everything " — the bartender handing me change of $10,
I stared at him amiably eyes thru an obvious Adamic beard —
with Montana musicians homeless in Manhattan, teen age
curly hair themselves — we sat at the antique booth & gossiped,
Madame Grady's literary salon a curious value in New York —
" If I had my way I'd cut off your hair and send you to Vietnam " —
" Bless you then " I replied to a hatted thin citizen hurrying to
    the barroom door
upon wet dark Amsterdam Avenue decades later —
"And if I couldn't do that I'd cut your throat" he snarled farewell,
and " Bless you sir " I added as he went to his fate in the rain,
    dapper Irishman.
April 1966

TO THE BODY

Enthroned in plastic, shrouded in wool, diamond crowned,
transported in aluminum, shoe'd in synthetic rubber, fed by
    asparagus, adored by all animals,
ear-lull'd by electric mantra rock, chemical roses acrid in the nose,
observant of large-nostril'd air factories, every crack of the
    skin kissed by beloved grandmothers,
so man woman child are tender meat become consciously genital
    with the shudder & blush of substance
adorned with hair at crotch and brain — beard on lion and
    youth by fireside.
June 15, 1966

CITY MIDNIGHT JUNK STRAINS

FOR FRANK O'HARA

Switch on lights yellow as the sun
                        in the bedroom ...
The gaudy poet dead   Frank O'Hara's bones
                        under cemetery grass
An emptiness at 8PM in the Cedar Bar
        Throngs of drunken
                guys talking about paint
        & lofts, and Pennsylvania youth.
                Kline attacked by his heart
& chattering Frank
                stopped forever —
    Faithful drunken adorers, mourn.
                The busfare's a nickle more
        past his old apartment 9th Street by the park.
Delicate Peter loved his praise,
        I wait for the things he says
                        about me —
        Did he think me an Angel
        as angel I am still talking into earth's microphone
                        willy nilly
                — to come back as words ghostly hued
                        by early death
        but written so bodied
                mature in another decade.
Chatty prophet
                of yr own loves, personal
                memory feeling fellow
        Poet of building-glass
I see you walking you said with your tie

flopped over your shoulder   in the wind down 5th Ave
    under the handsome breasted workmen
      on their scaffolds ascending Time
        & washing the windows of Life
— off to a date with Martinis & a blond
    beloved poet far from home
      — with thee and Thy sacred Metropolis
in the enormous bliss   of a long afternoon
where death is the shadow
    cast by Rockefeller Center
      over your intimate street.
Who were you, black suited, hurrying to meet,
    Unsatisfied one?
      Unmistakable,
        Darling date
for the charming solitary   young poet with a big cock
    who could fuck you all night long
      till you never came,
trying your torture on his   obliging fond body
eager to satisfy god's whim that made you
    Innocent,   as you are.
I tried   your boys and found them ready
    sweet and amiable
      collected gentlemen
        with large sofa apartments
lonesome to please   for pure language;
and you mixed with money
    because you knew enough language to be rich
      if you wanted your walls to be empty —
Deep philosophical terms dear Edwin Denby serious as Herbert Read
    with silvery hair   announcing your dead gift

to the grave crowd   whose historic op art   frisson was
the new sculpture your big blue wounded body made in the
                                   Universe
     when you went away   to Fire Island for the weekend
   tipsy with a family of decade-olden friends

Peter stares out the window   at robbers
        the Lower East Side   distracted in Amphetamine
I stare into my head   & look for your/ broken roman nose
       your wet mouth-smell of martinis
          & a big artistic tipsy kiss.
  40's only half a life   to have filled
        with so many fine parties and evenings'
          interesting drinks together with one
               faded friend or new
               understanding social cat . . .
I want to be there in your garden party in the clouds
              all of us naked
strumming our harps and reading each other   new poetry
   in the boring celestial
        friendship Committee Museum.
You're in a bad mood?
               Take an Aspirin.
           In the Dumps?
             I'm falling asleep
               safe in your thoughtful arms.
Someone uncontrolled by History would have to own Heaven,
               on earth as it is.
I hope you satisfied your childhood love
   Your puberty fantasy   your sailor punishment on your knees
             your mouth-suck

Elegant insistency
> on the honking self-prophetic Personal
> as Curator of funny emotions to the mob,
Trembling One, whenever possible. I see New York thru your eyes
> and hear of one funeral a year nowadays —
>> From Billie Holiday's time
> appreciated more and more
a common ear
> for our deep gossip.

July 29, 1966

HOLY GHOST ON THE NOD OVER THE BODY OF BLISS

Is this the God of Gods, the one I heard about
in memorized language Universities murmur?
Dollar bills can buy it ! the great substance
exchanges itself freely through all the world's
poetry money, past and future currencies
issued & redeemed by the identical bank,
electric monopoly after monopoly owl-eyed
on every one of 90 billion dollarbills vibrating
to the pyramid-top in the United States of Heaven —
Aye aye Sir Owl Oh say can you see in the dark you
observe Minerva nerveless in Nirvana because
Zeus rides reindeer thru Bethlehem's blue sky.
It's Buddha sits in Mary's belly waving Kuan
Yin's white hand at the Yang-tze that Mao sees,
tongue of Kali licking Krishna's soft blue lips.
Chango holds Shiva's prick, Ouroboros eats th'cobalt bomb,
Parvati on YOD's perfumèd knee cries Aum
& Santa Barbara rejoices in the alleyways of Brindaban
La Illaha El (lill) Allah Who — Allah Akbar !
Goliath struck down by kidneystone, Golgothas grow old,
All these wonders are crowded in the Mind's Eye
Superman & Batman race forward, Zarathustra on Coyote's ass,
Laotzu disappearing at the gate, God mocks God,
Job sits bewildered that Ramakrishna is Satan
and Bodhidharma forgot to bring Nothing.

December 1966

WALES VISITATION

White fog lifting & falling on mountain-brow
        Trees moving in rivers of wind
                    The clouds arise
   as on a wave, gigantic eddy lifting mist
     above teeming ferns exquisitely swayed
                  along a green crag
    glimpsed thru mullioned glass in valley raine —

Bardic, O Self, Visitacione, tell naught
   but what seen by one man in a vale in Albion,
     of the folk, whose physical sciences end in Ecology,
          the wisdom of earthly relations,
     of mouths & eyes interknit ten centuries visible
        orchards of mind language manifest human,
 of the satanic thistle that raises its horned symmetry
  flowering above sister grass-daisies' pink tiny
          bloomlets angelic as lightbulbs —

Remember 160 miles from London's symmetrical thorned tower
    & network of TV pictures flashing bearded your Self
 the lambs on the tree-nooked hillside this day bleating
 heard in Blake's old ear, & the silent thought of Wordsworth in
               eld Stillness
  clouds passing through skeleton arches of Tintern Abbey —
     Bard Nameless as the Vast, babble to Vastness !

All the Valley quivered, one extended motion, wind
        undulating on mossy hills

a giant wash that sank white fog delicately down red runnels
on the mountainside
whose leaf-branch tendrils moved asway
in granitic undertow down —
and lifted the floating Nebulous upward, and lifted the arms of the
trees
and lifted the grasses an instant in balance
and lifted the lambs to hold still
and lifted the green of the hill, in one solemn wave

A solid mass of Heaven, mist-infused, ebbs thru the vale,
a wavelet of Immensity, lapping gigantic through Llanthony
Valley,
the length of all England, valley upon valley under Heaven's ocean
tonned with cloud-hang,
— Heaven balanced on a grassblade.
Roar of the mountain wind slow, sigh of the body,
One Being on the mountainside stirring gently
Exquisite scales trembling everywhere in balance,
one motion thru the cloudy sky-floor shifting on the million
feet of daisies,
one Majesty the motion that stirred wet grass quivering
to the farthest tendril of white fog poured down
through shivering flowers on the mountain's
head —

No imperfection in the budded mountain,
Valleys breathe, heaven and earth move together,
daisies push inches of yellow air, vegetables tremble,
green atoms shimmer in grassy mandalas,
sheep speckle the mountainside, revolving their jaws with empty
eyes,
horses dance in the warm rain,

tree-lined canals network through live farmland,
blueberries fringe stone walls
on hill breasts nippled with hawthorn,
pheasants croak up meadow-bellies haired with fern —

Out, out on the hillside, into the ocean sound, into delicate
gusts of wet air,
Fall on the ground, O great Wetness, O Mother, No harm on
thy body!
Stare close, no imperfection in the grass,
each flower Buddha-eye, repeating the story,
the myriad-formed soul
Kneel before the foxglove raising green buds, mauve bells drooped
doubled down the stem trembling antennae,
& look in the eyes of the branded lambs that stare
breathing stockstill under dripping hawthorn —
I lay down mixing my beard with the wet hair of the mountainside,
smelling the brown vagina-moist ground, harmless,
tasting the violet thistle-hair, sweetness —
One being so balanced, so vast, that its softest breath
moves every floweret in the stillness on the valley floor,
trembles lamb-hair hung gossamer rain-beaded in the grass,
lifts trees on their roots, birds in the great draught
hiding their strength in the rain, bearing same weight,

Groan thru breast and neck, a great Oh! to earth heart
Calling our Presence together
The great secret is no secret
Senses fit the winds,
Visible is visible,
rain-mist curtains wave through the bearded vale,
grey atoms wet the wind's Kaballah

Crosslegged on a rock in dusk rain,
      rubber booted in soft grass, mind moveless,
  breath trembles in white daisies by the roadside,
          Heaven breath and my own symmetric
    Airs wavering thru antlered green fern
drawn in my navel, same breath as breathes thru Capel-Y-Ffn,
       Sounds of Aleph and Aum
           through forests of gristle,
    my skull and Lord Hereford's Knob equal,
              All Albion one.

What did I notice? Particulars! The
     vision of the great One is myriad —
  smoke curls upward from ash tray,
      house fire burned low,
The night, still wet & moody black heaven
              starless
  upward in motion with wet wind.

July 29, 1967 (LSD) — August 3, 1967 (London)

PENTAGON EXORCISM

"No taxation without representation"

Who represents my body in Pentagon? Who spends
my spirit's billions for war manufacture? Who
levies the majority to exult unwilling in Bomb
Roar? Brainwash! *Mind-fear! Governor's language!*
Military-Industrial-Complex! *President's language!*
Corporate voices jabber on electric networks building
body-pain, chemical ataxia, physical slavery
to diaphanoid Chinese Cosmic-eye Military Tyranny
movie hysteria — Pay my taxes? No Westmoreland wants
to be Devil, others die for his General Power
sustaining hurt millions in house security
tuning to images on TV's separate universe where
peasant manhoods burn in black & white forest
villages — represented less than myself by Magic
Intelligence influence matter-scientists' Rockefeller
bank telephone war investment Usury Agency
executives jetting from McDonnell Douglas *to* General Dynamics
over smog-shrouded metal-noised treeless cities
patrolled by radio fear with tear gas, businessman!
Go spend your bright billions for this suffering!
Pentagon wake from planet-sleep! Apokatastasis!
Spirit Spirit Dance Dance Spirit Spirit Dance!
Transform Pentagon skeleton to maiden-temple O Phantom
Guevara! Om Raksa Raksa Hum Hum Hum Phat Svaha!
Anger Control your Self feared Chaos, suffocation
body-death in Capitols caved with stone radar sentinels!

Back! Back! Back! Central Mind-machine Pentagon reverse consciousness! Hallucination manifest! A million Americas gaze out of man-spirit's naked Pentacle! Magnanimous reaction to signal Peking, isolate Space-beings!

Milan 9/29/67